IRAN'S
BALLISTIC
BUILDUP

The March Toward
Nuclear-Capable Missiles

Iran's Ballistic Buildup: The March Toward Nuclear-Capable Missiles

Copyright © National Council of Resistance of Iran – U.S. Representative Office, 2018.

First published in 2018 by
National Council of Resistance of Iran - U.S. Representative Office (NCRI-US), 1747 Pennsylvania Ave., NW, Suite 1125, Washington, DC 20006

ISBN-10 (hard cover): 1-944942-17-3
ISBN-13 (hard cover): 978-1-944942-17-5

ISBN-10 (paperback): 1-944942-15-7
ISBN-13 (paperback): 978-1-944942-15-1

ISBN-10 (eBook): 1-944942-16-5
ISBN-13 (eBook): 978-1-944942-16-8

Library of Congress Control Number: 2018940852

Library of Congress Cataloging-in-Publication Data

National Council of Resistance of Iran - U.S. Representative Office.
Iran's Ballistic Buildup: The March Toward Nuclear-Capable Missiles

1. Iran. 2. Ballistic Missiles. 3. Missiles. 4. Nuclear. 5. Middle East

First Edition: May 2018

Printed in the United States of America

Table of Contents

EXECUTIVE SUMMARY

E fforts and concerns to curb the strategic threats emanating from the Iranian regime's missiles program and their wider impact on geostrategic dynamics have become international in scope. States and state officials from a wide range of countries in the world, including in the Middle East, have raised grave alarm, leading the United Nations Security Council to take up the issue and adopt a number of decisions and resolutions.

A number of studies and research regarding Tehran's missile capabilities, including the interconnected technical dimensions, have been published by a variety of credible international institutions, which primarily explored the detailed technical and military aspects and particulars of the missile program.

The present report, on the other hand, surveys other facets of the regime's missile capabilities, including the underlying organization, structure, production and development infrastructure, launch facilities and the command centers operating inside Iran. This feature makes the report unique in nature, and reveals the clerical establishment's core objectives and intentions when it comes to expanding its missile program. It views the missile program not as an instrument of deterrence but as a strategic means of statecraft for the regime, tied to its aggressive aspirations of one day leading an Islamic fundamentalist block while intimidating and blackmailing other regional and international players.

The IRGC initiated the missile program in earnest in the mid-1980s with the procurement of Scud missiles. Referring to the regime's Lebanon-based terrorist proxy, the former IRGC minister Mohsen Rafiqdoost said in a September 25, 2016 speech that Hezbollah had been created by former supreme leader Khomeini to "Islamize" other countries in the region. "Today, in the era of the [Supreme] Leader [Ayatollah Ali Khamenei], Hezbollah has become a supreme force in the region," he stated.[1] Put simply, this, and similar statements, represent the conceptual model and ideological driver behind the regime's bourgeoning missile program.

It was on the backdrop of this ideology that Tehran approached international nuclear and missile experts, including those in North Korea, Libya, Syria and the infamous AQ Khan network in Pakistan. Khan is suspected of visiting the Iranian reactor at Bushehr in February 1986 and again in January 1987.[2]

By 1987, The New York Times reported that "American analysts and foreign diplomats in Teheran often cite the Revolutionary Guards' control of weapons production as a sign of the organization's growing influence over Iranian military affairs."[3]

---

[1] "We Have Warehouses Full [Of Missiles]," *Middle East Media Research Institute*, October 2, 2016. <https://www.memri.org/reports/iranian-official-if-america-wants-try-its-luck-against-us-it-should-know-we-are-completely>

[2] Michael Laufer, "AQ Khan Nuclear Chronology," *Carnegie Endowment for International Peace*, September 7, 2005. <https://carnegieendowment.org/2005/09/07/a.-q.-khan-nuclear-chronology-pub-17420>

[3] John H. Cushman Jr., "Iran Says It Is Expanding Its Ability to Make Arms," *The New York Times*, September 13, 1987. <https://www.nytimes.com/1987/09/13/world/iran-says-it-is-expanding-its-ability-to-make-arms.html>

This report has been complied on the basis of intelligence and information obtained by the main organized opposition, Mujahedin-e Khalq (MEK), from inside the Islamic Revolutionary Guard Corps (IRGC) and other regime military institutions leading the charge on missile development.

The opening chapters explore the organizational structure and make-up of institutions and organs involved in the development, application and storage of the various types of missiles possessed by the Iranian regime. They also expose the association and connections between the regime's missile activities on the one hand and its nuclear program on the other, including in particular their relations with North Korea.

Subsequent chapters examine international resolutions against the regime's missile activities, as well as the regime's clear violations of these resolutions as a result of missile exports, tests and also proxy attacks, particularly from Yemen.

Among the report's most significant conclusions are the following:

1. Increasing the scope of missile capabilities is a pillar of the clerical dictatorship's strategic military doctrine, especially after the Iran-Iraq War. This falls in conjunction with the necessity of acquiring nuclear weapons and expansion of non-conventional military tactics through the IRGC, the Bassij paramilitary force and other militias around the region.

2. Through its bourgeoning missile program, the IRGC intends to advance the regime's strategic policy of export of terrorism and fundamentalism, for which the missile program is a main pillar.

3. The manufacturing of ballistic missiles, with a maximum range of 2,000 km at present, is done with the sole

intention of developing a nuclear delivery system. The main organ overseeing the regime's missile development has an organic and unyielding relationship with Tehran's nuclear development organization, SPND (the Organization of Defensive Innovation and Research).

4. The IRGC is responsible for the development and application of missiles in recent years, and it has substantially expanded the program. The intricate web of institutions in this area are involved in various stages of production, storage, command, and launch under the oversight of the IRGC. This network advances the IRGC's main objectives under the supervision of Tehran's supreme leader Ali Khamenei.

5. The IRGC has obtained the technical know-how and a wealth of experience in the area of missile development from North Korea. It currently has close and systematic ties with the North's missile program.

6. The clerical regime fuels regional instability by illegally exporting missiles and missile technology to other countries like Yemen, Lebanon, Syria and Iraq, among others.

7. The 2017 and 2018 missile attacks conducted from Yemen against the country's neighbors occurred on the orders of the IRGC. The Houthi rebels in Yemen obtained the missiles from the IRGC.

8. After the July 2015 nuclear deal, in contradiction to the spirit of the agreement, the clerical regime increased the number of ballistic missile tests capable of carrying a nuclear load. Along with illicit exports to other players in the Middle East, which undermines regional security and stability, the regime seeks to compensate for its weakness as a result of temporarily backtracking from attempts to acquire a nuclear weapon.

INTRODUCTION

I n 1979, Ruhollah Khomeini hijacked the democratic revolution in Iran, leading the Iranian people into a dark period of religious fundamentalism and ideological extremism. To maintain his grasp on the nation, Khomeini ordered the creation of the Islamic Revolutionary Guard Corps (IRGC). The IRGC has kept the religious dictatorship in power through internal repression, fundamentalist propaganda, and the exportation of terrorism and war outside of Iran's borders.[4] Arguably, the most important tool in the IRGC's macabre arsenal is the regime's missile program.

The expansion of the IRGC's missile capabilities forms one of the three strategic pillars of the regime's military doctrine after the Iran-Iraq war of the 1980s. These three pillars are the development of nuclear weapons, obtaining long-range ballistic missiles, and expanding the regime's influence through unconventional warfare.

In order to advance this military strategy, the IRGC began procuring and importing technology for the production of ballistic missiles capable of carrying a nuclear warhead. In the past, the

---

[4] For its role in international terrorism, the IRGC has been placed under sanctions in accordance with several U.S. executive orders. In October 2017, the IRGC was sanctioned under Executive Order 13224 as an entity that supports international terrorism.

IRGC has used missiles to trigger regional conflicts and as a key instrument for meddling in the affairs of other countries in the region. In addition to exporting a variety of missiles to other regional actors, the IRGC has set up missile factories in Syria, Lebanon and Iraq in order to enlarge its sphere of influence.[5]

While the IRGC's missile activities have been sanctioned repeatedly by the United Nations Security Council (UNSC) and the United States Treasury Department, the IRGC has continued to rely on a range of illicit methods to procure parts and equipment through international smuggling networks.[6]

The Iranian regime's production and proliferation of nuclear capable ballistic missiles is intended to intimidate neighboring countries as part of the regime's designs for regional hegemony. Conventional cruise missiles, such as the Soumar and Qader, could be used to confront ships that pass through the Gulf of Oman and the Persian Gulf and threaten international shipping. Rockets, such as the Naze'at and the Fajr, are provided to proxy groups like Hamas, Hezbollah and the Yemeni Houthis, all of which are engaged in protracted conflicts in their respective countries.

Grasping the IRGC's missiles activities enables us to better comprehend the conduct of the *velayat-e faqih*, or absolute clerical rule, of the dictatorship and its IRGC backbone.

A cursory review of the missile program clarifies the role of the IRGC's aerospace organization in launching conflicts and triggering instability throughout the Middle East.

---

[5] Isabel Kershner, "Iran Building Weapons Factories in Syria and Lebanon, Israel Says," New York Times, August 29, 2017, https://www.nytimes.com/2017/08/29/world/middleeast/iran-missiles-lebanon-israel-.html.

[6] U.S. Department of the Treasury, 2017, "Treasury Sanctions Supporters Of Iran's Ballistic Missile Program And Iran's Islamic Revolutionary Guard Corps – Qods Force," https://www.treasury.gov/press-center/press-releases/Pages/as0004.aspx.

1

The IRGC's Missile Program: A Brief History

The formation of the IRGC's missile unit

In 1979, Khomeini established the Islamic Revolutionary Guard Corps (IRGC) despite the existence of the official armed forces. While a traditional military is tasked with protecting state borders, the IRGC's forces were organized with the intention of preserving the rule of the clergy and to export crises outside of Iran. With the start of the Iran-Iraq war in September 1980, the IRGC witnessed a dramatic expansion in its ranks and was equipped with heavy weaponry.

The IRGC became an official ministry of the Iranian government in 1983 and was made responsible for arranging war logistics during the Iran-Iraq conflict. The IRGC ministry was later integrated into the Defense Ministry. At the time, the Defense Ministry was under the control of army commanders. However, following the merger of the two, the Defense Ministry came under the control of senior IRGC commanders who usurped power from their former superiors. By 1984, the IRGC launched a wide-ranging effort to procure Scud missiles.

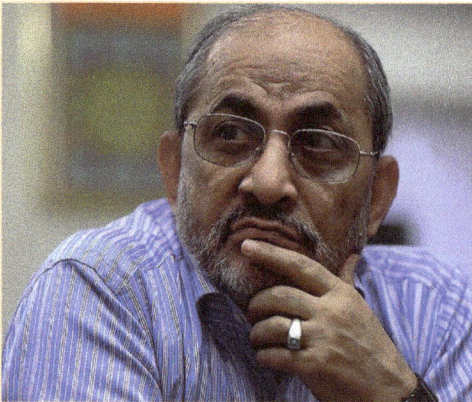

Mohsen Rafiqdoust met with the leaders of Libya and Syria to negotiate and reach an agreement to provide the regime with Scud missiles.

In interviews with state-run media, Mohsen Rafiqdoust[7], the first IRGC minister, provided a detailed description of the regime's attempts to purchase weapons and missiles from Libya, Syria, and North Ko-

---

[7] "Mohsen Rafiqdoost: We had to put on the Eastern Arms to Base the Base," BBC News, Last Modified September 26, 2016, http://www.bbc.com/persian/iran/2016/09/160926_l12_iran_sepah_rafighdoost.

rea. In July 1984, Rafiqdoust traveled to Libya and Syria where then Syrian president Hafez Assad agreed to train the IRGC in missile launches while former Libyan president Muammar Gaddafi reached an agreement to provide the regime with Scud missiles.

In November 1984, 13 individuals from the IRGC's artillery unit led by Hassan Tehrani Moqaddam[8] travelled to Syria to receive training on the launch of Scud B missiles. Three months later the first IRGC missile unit was created at Montazeri Garrison in Kermanshah (western Iran). In 1985, the IRGC commenced operations after purchasing Scud B missiles from Libya. In 1987, the missile section of the IRGC was reorganized within the IRGC air force. The new missile brigade was called the Seventh al-Hadid.

As for ballistic missiles, starting in July 1987 to March 1988, the IRGC purchased approximately 90 to 100 surface-to-surface missiles from North Korea, worth over $500M.

By the time the Iran-Iraq War drew to a close in 1988, the Iranian regime's missile organization had been separated from the traditional army chain of command and fallen fully under the authority of the IRGC, because the program's aggressive nature aligned more closely with the IRGC's *raison d'être*.

The expansion of the missile unit as part of the regime's post-war military strategy

Subsequent to the 1988 ceasefire in the Iran-Iraq war, the Iranian regime adopted a new strategy to maintain

---

[8]   David E. Sanger and William J. Broad, "Explosion Seen as Big Setback to Iran's Missile Program," *New York Times,* December 4, 2011, https://www.nytimes.com/2011/12/05/world/middleeast/blast-leveling-base-seen-as-big-setback-to-iran-missiles.html

regional influence. In light of the weakened air force, an essential element of this strategy was the acquiring of missile technology. In line with this objective, the IRGC kick-started a project to produce surface-to-surface missiles, which included various dimensions of research, development, manufacturing and assembly.

Obtaining missile production technology from North Korea

The IRGC sought to acquire missile technology by hiring experts inside Iran and obtaining information and technical know-how from China, North Korea and Russia. Brigadier General Manteqi, then head of the missile industry of the Defense Industries Organization initiated technological relations with North Korea for the transfer of missile technology after he visited the country with a 21-member delegation in 1993. They signed agreements with North Korea and China, enabling the regime to acquire missile technology.[9]

Aerospace Industries Organization created to expand production

To step up production efforts, the Iranian regime created an independent organization for the manufacturing of missiles in 1996, entitled the Aerospace Industries Organization (AIO) within the Ministry of Defense and Armed Forces Logistics (MODAFL). Brigadier General Mehrdad Akhlaghi

---

[9] David Sanger, "Missile is tested by North Koreans," *The New York Times,* June 13, 1993, https://www.nytimes.com/1993/06/13/world/missile-is-tested-by-north-koreans.html; Anthony H. Cordesman and Adam C. Seitz. "Iranian Weapons of Mass Destruction: Capabilities, Developments, and Strategic Uncertainties," *Center for Strategic and International Studies,* October 14, 2008.

is the AIO commander with the mandate of producing and proliferating ballistic missiles. Akhlaghi whose name was listed on UN Security Council Resolution 1747 in 2007, is currently sanctioned by the U.S. Treasury Department.[10] In addition to surface-to-surface missiles, this organization is involved in the production of other weaponry such as surface-to-air missiles, anti-ship missiles, and surface-to-sea missiles. Both the Imam Hussein University and Malek Ashtar University cooperate with the AIO to research the development of ballistic missiles. The AIO manufactures the missiles and supplies them to the IRGC missile unit.

The AIO has eight independent groups for the production of various missile types.

Ballistic missiles capable of carrying nuclear warheads

The Organization of Defensive Innovation and Research (*Sazman-e Pazhouheshhaye Novin-e* Defa'i), known by its Farsi acronym, SPND, is responsible for designing the nuclear warhead for Shahab 3 missiles. Documents obtained by the International Atomic Energy Agency (IAEA) and periodic reports later released by the UN watchdog from 2005 to 2016 provide more details in this regard.[11] According to the IAEA, "Iran considered a number of technical options for a fuzing, arming and firing system that would ensure that the new Shahab 3 missile spherical payload would remain safe until

---

[10] Mehrdad Akhlaghi, also known as Mehrdad Akhlaghi Ketabchi is designated under OFAC's Sanctions List for Weapons of Mass Destruction Proliferators Sanctions Regulations, 31 C.F.R. part 544 (NPWMD), Iranian Financial Sanctions Regulations, 31 CFR part 561 (IFSR), https://sanctionssearch.ofac.treas.gov/Details.aspx?id=1950

[11] "IAEA and Iran - IAEA Reports," *International Atomic Energy Agency*, https://www.iaea.org/newscenter/focus/iran/iaea-and-iran-iaea-reports.

the re-entry vehicle reached its designated target, and that the payload would then function correctly."[12]

The formation of the IRGC Aerospace Force to expand the IRGC's missile program

Initially, the IRGC only had ground forces. In 1985, on Khomeini's orders, it created a naval force and an air force as well. Since then, the missile unit became part of its air force. To enlarge the scope of the Iranian regime's nuclear activities, the IRGC restructured its organization and in September 2009, the IRGC "air force" became the "aerospace force."

The structure of the aerospace force includes the IRGC air force, missile and anti-aircraft units. All of the regime's missiles are essentially under the control of these missile units.

---

[12] Director General, "Final Assessment on Past and Present Outstanding Issues regarding Iran's Nuclear Programme," GOV/2015/68, December 2, 2015, https://www.iaea.org/sites/default/files/gov-2015-68.pdf.

CURRENT CAPABILITIES

Below are some of the missile types produced by the IRGC. The main surface-to-surface IRGC missiles can be summarized using the following categories:

1. **MEDIUM-RANGE BALLISTIC MISSILES:** These missiles include Shahab 3, Sejil, Qadr, Ashura and some of the missiles that launch satellites into space, such as Safir. These missiles all have a range between 1,500 km to 2,000 km and have the capability to carry a nuclear warhead. Despite a ban on the regime using these types of missiles by UN Security Council Resolution 2231, the IRGC continues to launch these missiles on Khamenei's orders.[13]

2. **OTHER MISSILE TYPES:** The remaining types of missiles produced by the IRGC are modeled after North Korean, Chinese or Russian missiles. They include short-range surface-to-surface, sea and anti-aircraft missiles. Some of these missiles include Fateh 110, Saeqeh, Zelzal, and Nazeat. The regime has shipped these missiles to Syria, Yemen, Iraq, Lebanon and Afghanistan for use by its proxies. It has also used them to threaten shipping in the Persian Gulf and the Gulf of Oman.

---

[13] "Missiles of Iran," Missile Threat; *Center for Strategic and International Studies Missile Defense Project*, https://missilethreat.csis.org/country/iran/.

Brig. Gen. Amir Ali Hajizadeh, the commander of the IRGC Aerospace Force, said on November 11, 2014: "The missile manufacturing plants in Syria have been transferred to them from Iran.[14]

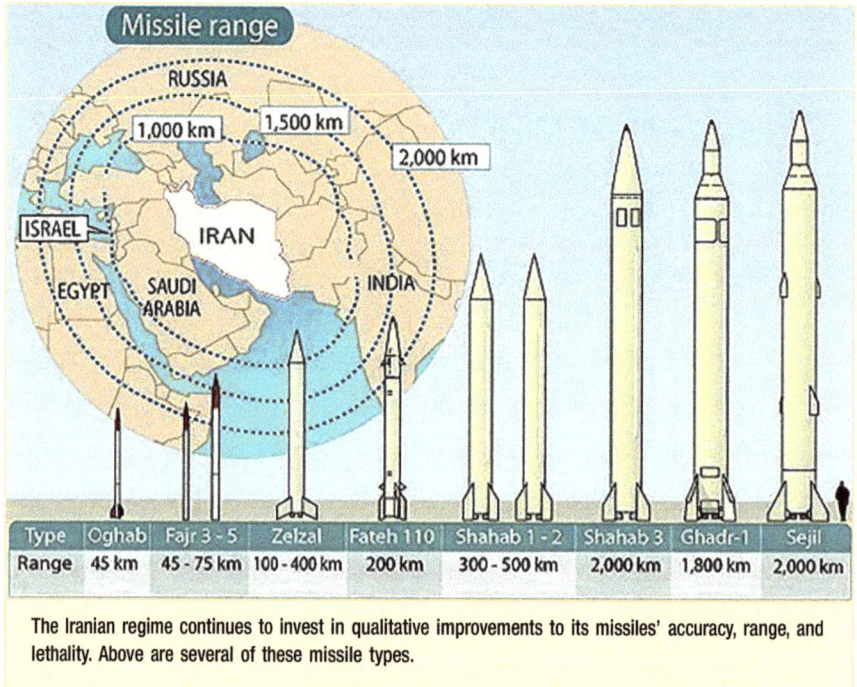

Type	Oghab	Fajr 3 - 5	Zelzal	Fateh 110	Shahab 1 - 2	Shahab 3	Ghadr-1	Sejil
Range	45 km	45 - 75 km	100 - 400 km	200 km	300 - 500 km	2,000 km	1,800 km	2,000 km

The Iranian regime continues to invest in qualitative improvements to its missiles' accuracy, range, and lethality. Above are several of these missile types.

---

14 "Commander: Syrian Missile-Manufacturing Plants Built by Iran," *Fars News Agency*, Nov 11. 2014, http://en.farsnews.com/newstext. aspx?nn=13930820000325.

2

IRGC's Aerospace Force

Mission — The IRGC's aerospace force has several mandates: an aggressive (assault) mandate using warplanes and missile units; a defensive mandate using anti-aircraft units and artillery; a reconnaissance mandate using planes, helicopters, drones and electronic surveillance; and an air logistics mandate carried out through air transport, airborne and heliborne operations.

COMMANDER: The commander of the aerospace force is IRGC Brig. Gen. Amir Ali Hajizadeh.[15]

LOCATION: Dastvareh Garrison located in northwestern Tehran near Chitgar Park.

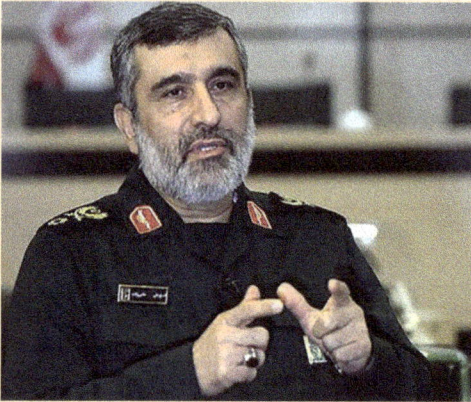

TEHRAN (FNA) — Commander of the Islamic Revolution Guards Corps (IRGC) Aerospace Force Brigadier General Amir Ali Hajizadeh, stresses continued progress in the regime's defense field.

ORGANIZATION AT A GLANCE:

- ☑ 15 divisions and command centers
- ☑ 9 air bases
- ☑ Surface-to-surface missile units
- ☑ Anti-aircraft units

---

[15] "Iran self-sufficient in producing missiles, drones, smart bombs: IRGC commander," *Press TV,* July 18, 2017, http://www.presstv.com/Detail/2017/07/18/528885/Iran-US-Syria-IRGC-Aerospace-Division-Amir-Ali-Hajizadeh-Daesh-Dayr-alZawr-Qods-Headquarters.

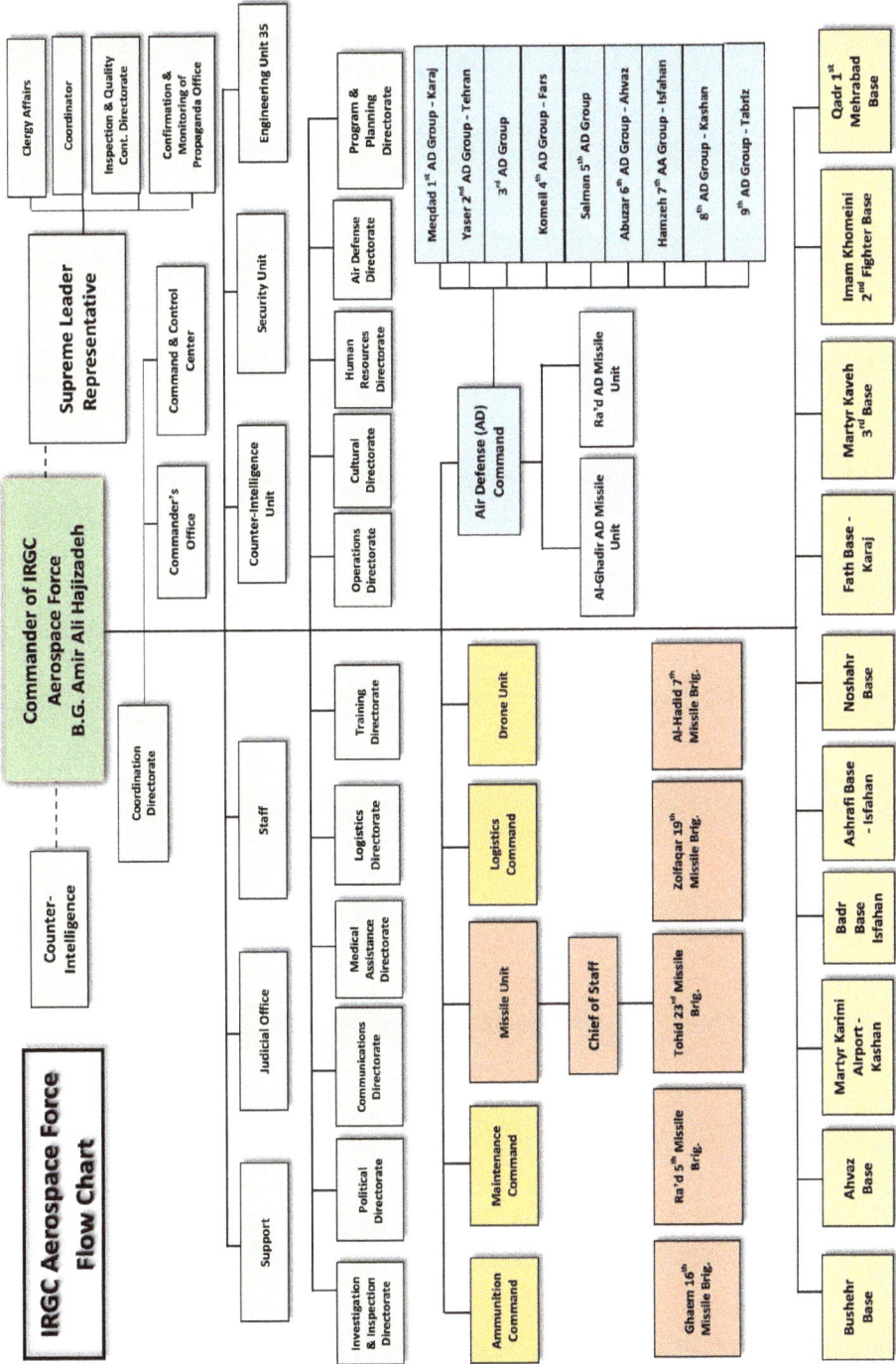

IRGC Aerospace Force Flow Chart

- Clergy Affairs
- Coordinator
- Inspection & Quality Cont. Directorate
- Confirmation & Monitoring of Propaganda Office

Supreme Leader Representative

Commander of IRGC Aerospace Force B.G. Amir Ali Hajizadeh

- Counter-Intelligence

- Coordination Directorate

- Engineering Unit 35
- Security Unit
- Command & Control Center
- Commander's Office
- Counter-Intelligence Unit

Directorates:
- Program & Planning Directorate
- Air Defense Directorate
- Human Resources Directorate
- Cultural Directorate
- Operations Directorate

Air Defense (AD) Command
- Ra'd AD Missile Unit
- Al-Ghadir AD Missile Unit

AD Groups:
- Meqdad 1st AD Group – Karaj
- Yaser 2nd AD Group – Tehran
- 3rd AD Group
- Komeil 4th AD Group – Fars
- Salman 5th AD Group
- Abuzar 6th AD Group – Ahvaz
- Hamzeh 7th AA Group – Isfahan
- 8th AD Group – Kashan
- 9th AD Group – Tabriz

Support / Staff:
- Support
- Judicial Office
- Staff
- Investigation & Inspection Directorate
- Political Directorate
- Communications Directorate
- Medical Assistance Directorate
- Logistics Directorate
- Training Directorate

Commands / Units:
- Ammunition Command
- Maintenance Command
- Missile Unit
- Logistics Command
- Drone Unit
- Chief of Staff

Missile Brigades:
- Ghaem 16th Missile Brig.
- Ra'd 5th Missile Brig.
- Tohid 23rd Missile Brig.
- Zolfaqar 19th Missile Brig.
- Al-Hadid 7th Missile Brig.

Bases:
- Bushehr Base
- Ahvaz Base
- Martyr Karimi Airport – Kashan
- Badr Base Isfahan
- Ashrafi Base – Isfahan
- Noshahr Base
- Fath Base – Karaj
- Martyr Kaveh 3rd Base
- Imam Khomeini 2nd Fighter Base
- Qadr 1st Mehrabad Base

MISSILE UNIT OF THE IRGC AEROSPACE FORCE

The missile unit is the most important section of the IRGC's aerospace force. The command center of the IRGC's missile unit is located at the Dastvareh Garrison, situated near Karaj highway north of Chitgar park. The IRGC aerospace organization has several missile groups. Five of the most important groups or brigades include:

- ☑ 7th al-Hadid missile brigade: This brigade is equipped with Scud B and Scud C (Shahab 1 and Shahab 2) missiles. It is the oldest missile brigade of the Iranian regime and is located at the al-Mahdi Garrison in Bidganeh village in the Fardis district of Karaj. North Korean missile experts provided training at this garrison. A portion of the garrison is dedicated to missile storage, while another portion is used for missile repairs and maintenance.

- ☑ 19th Zolfaqar missile brigade: One of the centers of this brigade is situated at Sajjad Garrison near Bidganeh village near Karaj.

- ☑ 23rd Towhid missile brigade: This brigade was previously located at a garrison called Nour al-Mahdi in Tehran, on the Qom highway. However, since 2001, it has been relocated to Khorramabad at a garrison situated in the mountains.

- ☑ 15th Qa'em missile group: Created in 2000, this group is a unit dedicated to surface- to-surface missiles. Its forces are located at Javad al-a'ameh Garrison in the city of Shiraz, Fars Province.

- ☑ 5th Raad missile group: This group was created in 2000. It oversees Shahab-3 missiles. One of the centers of the 5th Raad missile group is located at the Sajjad Garrison in Bidganeh village in the Fardis district of Karaj.

Death of Hassan Tehrani Moqaddam, commander of the IRGC's missile unit

When the IRGC's missile unit was created in 1985, Hassan Tehrani Moqaddam[16] was appointed as its commander, a post that he held until his death on November 20, 2011. He was also the commander of the IRGC air force missile unit. Tehrani Moqaddam was a key figure, both as a technical ex-

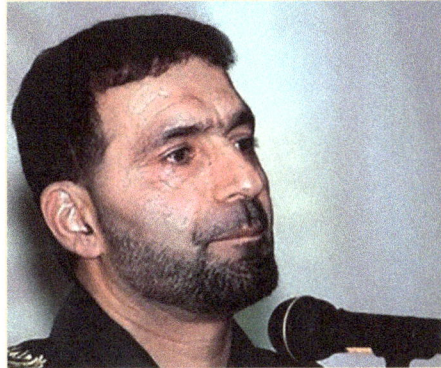

Hassan Tehrani Moqaddam deceased in 2011 at the Bidganeh arsenal explosion.

pert as well as a commander, and held the post for 28 years. He was trained on using missiles in Syria, and missile manufacturing technology by North Korean experts. Tehrani Moqaddam was killed along with a number of the IRGC's missile experts while working on the final stages of assembling a ballistic missile, as a result of an explosion caused by

---

[16] "Mohsen Rafiqdoost: We had to put on the Eastern Arms to Base the Base," *BBC News,* September 26, 2016, http://www.bbc.com/persian/iran/2016/09/160926_l12_iran_sepah_rafighdoost.

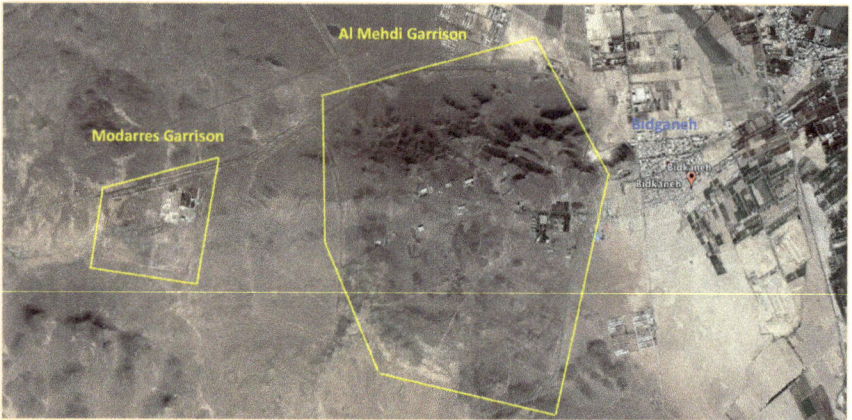

Modarres and Al-Mehdi Garrisons; the explosion took place at Modarres Garrison

disruptions in the missile-related electrical grid.[17] The blast, which occurred at Modarres Garrison, was so loud that it was heard in eastern Tehran, as debris from explosion at the garrison were seen scattered kilometers away.

Modarres Garrison before 2011 explosion, which killed Hassan Tehrani Moqaddam

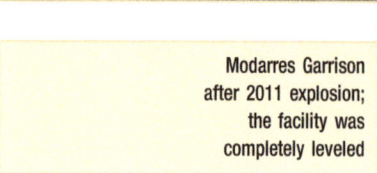

Modarres Garrison after 2011 explosion; the facility was completely leveled

---

[17] Douglas Birch, "Iran Group Claims Blast Hit Missile Base, Not Ammo Depot," *The Seattle Times*, November 14, 2011, https://www.seattletimes.com/nation-world/iran-group-claims-blast-hit-missile-base-not-ammo-depot/.

FOUR KEY MISSILE CENTERS OF THE IRGC AEROSPACE FORCE

The Semnan Missile Center:

This is the largest missile complex in Iran. It is located 70 km southeast of the city of Semnan in a relatively mountainous region. The complex is comprised of several sections, which include a command center, launching pads for medium-range missiles, explosive testing sites and a training facility. In recent years, most of the regime's missile tests have been conducted at this location.

This center has been actively collaborating with SPND, the organization tasked with building a nuclear bomb.

SPND is the Farsi acronym of the engineering unit tasked with the development of nuclear weapons inside the Iranian regime. Its full name is the Organization of Defensive Innovation and Research (*Sazman-e Pazhouheshhaye Novin-e Defa'i*). The National Council of Resistance of Iran first revealed the existence of SPND in July 2011 in Washington, DC.[18] Three years later, on August 29, 2014, SPND was designated by the U.S. Department of State under Executive Order (E.O.)

---

[18] "Opposition: Iran consolidates nuclear bomb effort," Associated Press, last modified July 23, 2011, http://usatoday30.usatoday.com/news/washington/2011-07-23-iran-nuclear-program_n.htm

13382.[19] The head of SPND is Mohsen Fakhrizadeh Mahabadi, also known as Dr. Hassan Mohseni, a veteran IRGC brigadier general and the key figure in the regime's nuclear weapons program.

On a weekly basis, a group with high security clearance, under the command of Brig. Gen. Mostafa Siri, commander of SPND intelligence security, visits the Semnan center. (The Iranian resistance revealed in 2008 the connection between the nuclear arms manufacturing organization and Hemmat Missile Industry Group in the field of manufacturing nuclear warhead).[20]

The Tehran regime has often referred to the existence of "missile cities."[21] The Semnan missile center is one of these locations.

General Area of Semnan Missile Site southeast of Semnan

---

[19] Exec. Order No. 13382, 3 C.F.R. (2005).

[20] David Brunnstrom, "Iranian Dissidents Urge Immediate Nuclear Checks," *Reuters,* February 20, 2008, https://www.reuters.com/article/idUSL2016528.

[21] Peter Kenyon, "Iran Offers A Rare Peek At An Underground 'Missile City," *NPR,* January 7, 2016, https://www.npr.org/sections/parallels/2016/01/07/462248223/iran-offers-a-rare-peek-at-an-underground-missile-city.

Various Locations at Semnan Missile Site

A-Control and Command Center-Semnan

Testing and Launching Pad B

Testing and Launching Pad C

Complex D of Logistics and Security Facilities at Semnan Missile Site

Complex E of Logistics and Security Facilities at Semnan Missile Site

Complex F of Logistics and Security Facilities at Semnan Missile Site

The Lar Missile Center:

This site is located approximately 6 km west of Lar city in a mountainous region, in the southern province of Fars. It has an extensive array of tunnels and underground facilities. Severe security conditions are imposed in this region. There is a kiosk and a barricade at the entrance of the mountainous area with military forces stationed there. Cell phones are disconnected on the way to this center and are banned within its perimeter.

The Lar missile center is one of the regime's primary missile centers that Tehran has described as part of its "missile cities."

General area of Lar City with the Lar Missile Center encircled

Lar Missile Center in Fars Province

Lar Missile Center in Fars Province including underground tunnels

Khorramabad Missile Center at Imam Ali Garrison:

This garrison is located 25 km west of Khorramabad city toward Koohdasht and on the foothills of Sefid Kouh Mountains, in the western province of Lorestan. The area is completely surrounded by mountains. The regime uses this garrison to launch Shahab-3 missiles. In 2010, an accidental explosion of a Shahab-3 missile during a test resulted in the deaths of 20 individuals at this location.[22]

The Khatam al Anbia Construction Headquarters of the IRGC has launched two extensive tunnel construction projects in the area. The director of the IRGC's confidential plans in charge of executing this project is an engineer named Bassami.

General area of Khorramabad with the Imam Ali Garrison marked on the map

---

[22] Thomas Erdbink, "Members of Iran Revolutionary Guard Killed in Ammunition Blast," Washington Post, October 12, 2010, http://www.washingtonpost.com/wp-dyn/content/article/2010/10/12/AR2010101203356.html.

Bassami also led the Fordow tunnel projects, an integral part of the regime's hidden nuclear program.[23]

According to the NCRI's information, some of the IRGC's foreign experts also participated in the construction of this missile center.

Khorramabad Missile Center at Imam Ali Garrison

---

[23] "Fordow Fuel Enrichment Plant (FFEP)," ISIS Nuclear Iran, http://www.isisnucleariran.org/sites/detail/fordow/.

The complex of missile bases in the vicinity of Bidganeh Village near Karaj city:

The garrisons and bases of this region are the oldest missile units. The Al-Mahdi and Sajjad garrisons are locations where the IRGC's missile brigades are stationed. They also contain storage facilities for the regime's ballistic missiles.

The regime has built extensive underground facilities for the storage of the missiles in these two garrisons. The Modarres

Al-Mahdi Garrison-Bidganeh

Sajjad Garrison-Bidganeh

Modarres Garrison

Garrison, which is adjacent to the Al-Mahdi Garrison, is where the IRGC carries out its research on ballistic missiles.

In November 2011, 40 officers of the IRGC, including Brig. Gen. Hassan Tehrani Moghaddam, the father of the missile program of the Iranian regime, were killed by an explosion of one of the ballistic missiles in Modarres Garrison.[24]

---

[24] "Blast Kills Commander at Iran Base," *The New York Times*, November 13, 2011, https://www.nytimes.com/2011/11/14/world/middleeast/iran-blast-kills-revolutionary-guards-commander-at-base.html.

Missile Centers Across Iran Associated

NO	BASE CENTER	GOV. BODY	SUBJECT
1	Dastvareh Base	IRGC Aerospace	IRGC Aerospace Command Staff & Missile Unit Command
2	Al-Mahdi Base	Al-Hadid 7th Missile Group	Al-Hadid 7th Missile Group Base
3	Sajjad Base	Raad 5th Missile Group	Base for Raad 5th and Zolfeqar 9th Missile Groups
4	Imam Ali Base (Khorram Abad Missile Center)	Tohid 23rd and Al-hadid 7th Missile Groups	Depot and Launching Site for Shahab 3 Missiles
5	Javadol Aema Base	Ghaem 15th Missile Group	Base for Ghaem 15th Missile Group and Missile Arsenal
6	Lar Missile Center	IRGC Aerospace Force	Missile Arsenal and Launching Site for Missiles
7	Semnan Missile Base	IRGC Aerospace Force	Missile Arsenal, Research Center and Launching Site, One of the Biggest Missile Centers
8	Hemmat Montazeri	Part of Al-Hadid 7th Missile Group	Launching Site
9	Noor Al-Mahdi Base	Tohid 23rd Missile Group	Missile Base & AA Defense
10	Modarres Base	Missile Unit	Missile Unit Heavy Transport&Missile Research
11	Garmdarreh (Fajr) Base	Missile Unit	Large Installations and Underground Tunnels
12	Kosar (Panj Ghal'eh)	Missile Unit	Missile Unit
13	Missile Base	IRGC Aerospace Force	Missile Arsenal
14	Missile Base	IRGC Aerospace Force	Missile Arsenal
15	Missile Base	IRGC Navy	Missile Arsenal & Launching Site

with Aerospace Force of the IRGC

LOCATION	TYPE OF ACTIVITY	NOTES
Karaj Highway, adjacent to national park	Command	General Command of IRGC Aerospace Force, Command Post of Missile Units, Training and Accommodation of Commanders
West of Bidganeh Village, Mallard, Karaj	Manpower, Arsenal	Arsenal, Site for Manpower and Training, N. Korean Trainers Were Here
Bidganeh Village, 5 km to Al-Mahdi	Manpower, Arsenal	Arsenal, Manpower, Primary Missile Site
Sefid Kooh Area, km 25 Khorram Abad - Kooh Dasht Highway	Manpower, Arsenal, Launch	Large Site, Launching Site for Shahab 3, Big Explosion in 2010 Left 18 Dead
Shiraz, Fars Province	Manpower, Arsenal	Manpower, Tunnels for Missiles
6 km West of Lar City	Arsenal, Launch	The location of the 2nd Missile City with Numerous Tunnels
70 km Southeast of Semnan City	Research, Arsenal, Launch	Most Important Missile Center with Extensive Installations, Ballistic Missiles Test Site (missile city)
Kenesht Mountain Pass, Kermanshah	Manpower, Arsenal, Launch	Launching Site for Missiles Fired on Baghdad and Camp Ashraf
Adjacent to Fordo Nuclear Site, Tehran - Qom Highway	Arsenal, Air Defense, Previous Launch Site	
West of Al-Mahdi Base, Close to Bidganeh Village, Mallard, Karaj	Research, Arsenal	Explosion in 2011 while Preparing Missiles Left 40 dead
North of Garmdarreh, km 20 Tehran - Karaj Highway	Arsenal	Extensive Tunnels Built in Recent Years
Opposite Boroojerdi Base, Kermanshah	Arsenal, Probable Launch Site	Arsenal
Mountains north of Isfahan, Delijan - Isfahan Highway	Arsenal, Probable Launch Site	Site for Extensive Tunnels and Installations
Tabriz	Arsenal	Extensive Installations, Two Sets of Tunnels Titled Isar 2 and Isar 4
Qeshm Island	Arsenal, Launch	Underground Arsenal

NO	BASE CENTER	GOV. BODY	SUBJECT
16	Missile Base	IRGC Navy	Missile Arsenal & Launching Site
17	Missile Base	IRGC Navy	Missile Arsenal
18	Missile Base	IRGC Aerospace Force	Missile Arsenal
19	Missile Base	IRGC Aerospace Force	Training Site & Manpower
20	Missile and Other Weapons Center	IRGC Navy	Navy Missile Arsenal
21	Missile and Other Weapons Center	IRGC Navy	Navy Missile Arsenal
22	Missile and Other Weapons Center	IRGC Navy	Navy Missile Arsenal
23	Missile and Other Weapons Center	IRGC Navy	Navy Missile Arsenal
24	Missile and Launch Center	IRGC Aerospace Force	Missile Arsenal & Launching Site
25	IRGC Aerospace Base	IRGC Aerospace Force	Manpower, Training Site & Missile Arsenal
26	IRGC Missile Center	IRGC Aerospace Force	Missile Arsenal
27	IRGC Base	IRGC Aerospace Force	Missile Arsenal

LOCATION	TYPE OF ACTIVITY	NOTES
Great Tunb and Little Tunb Islands	Arsenal, Launch	Underground Arsenal
Jam City, Bushehr	Arsenal, Launch	Tunnels for IRGC Missiles
Gasr Firoozeh Mountains	Arsenal	Extensive Installations under Hills Southeast of Tehran
Badineh Village, Varamin, Southeast of Tehran	Manpower, Training	Close to an IRGC Qods Force Terrorist Training Site
Bidzard Area, Near Tunnel of Shiraz	Arsenal	Several Tunnels Built by IRGC Air Force Engineering (Ghorb Ghaem)
Outskirts of Borazjan	Arsenal	Tunnels for Missiles Arsenal
Outskirts of Bandar Abbas	Arsenal, Launch	Tunnels Built by IRGC Engineering
A Tunnel outskirts of Aslooyeh with 5 branches	Arsenal, Launch	Several Tunnels Built by IRGC Air Force Engineering
Kooh Siah Region, Southeast of Tehran	Arsenal, Previous Launch Site	IRGC's Former Missiles Test Site During 90s
SW Tehran, between Hasan Abad Mostowfi & Hasan Abad	Arsenal, Manpower	
Gatvand, Khuzestan	Arsenal	Tunnels Built by IRGC Engineering
Outskirts of Hamadan	Arsenal, Manpower	IRGC Missile Center for a Long Time

THE IRANIAN REGIME'S
MISSILE SITES

Locations of 42 Iranian Regime Missile Sites
Across the Country

Missile Site Locations in Central Iran

Missile Site Locations in Southern Iran

Missile Site Locations in Western Iran

The Command Headquarters of the IRGC Aerospace Force

Dastvareh Garrison next to Chitgar Park

Garmdarreh (Fajr) Base

The Garmdarreh missile base has large installations and underground tunnels. Extensive tunnels were built in recent years. It is located at the km 20 exit of Tehran-Karaj Highway.

Garmdarreh missile base with large underground tunnels

The Nouralmahdi Missile Site near Fordow

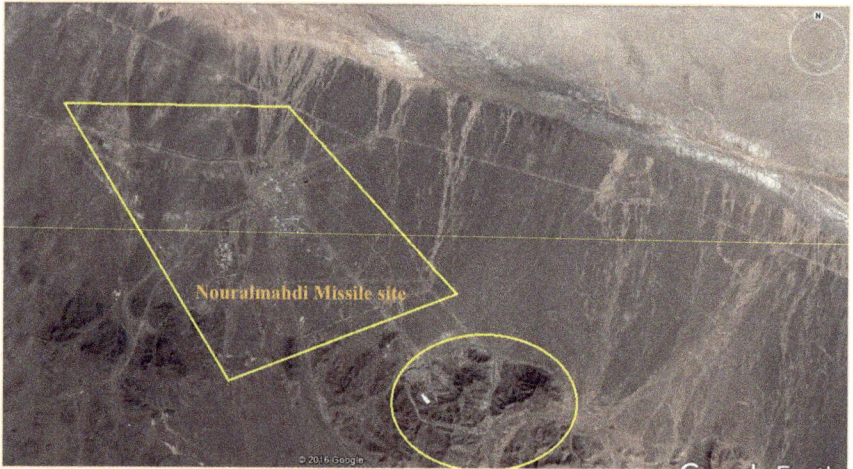

The missile site is near Fordow, the under-the-mountains uranium enrichment facility

Badindeh Missile Site in Varamin

Badindeh site near Varamin city south of Tehran

3

IRGC Missile Production Unit

Aerospace Industries Organization

n 1996, the IRGC created the Defense Ministry's Aerospace Industries Organization (AIO), in order to start domestic ballistic missile production lines.[25] The related technology was transferred to Iran from North Korea.

The AIO is responsible for the manufacturing of advanced missiles and other military industrial equipment and products. This includes responsibility for the production of surface-to-air missiles, surface-to-surface missiles, missiles launched from submarines, surface-to-sea missiles, sea-to-surface missiles as well as rockets and explosives, missile launch pads, gyroscopes and other equipment.

The AIO has ten departments and eight industrial groups for weapons manufacturing with over 30 facilities responsible for manufacturing components of missiles, military equipment and missile assembly (montage). The Shahab 3 missile and a variety of other advanced missiles are produced by industries tied to the AIO.

The AIO is located at Nobonyad Square in Tehran. However, its facilities are scattered in the Parchin region, Tehran suburbs, as well as other cities around the country.

Brigadier General Mehrdad Akhlaghi is the AIO commander.

---

[25] Since the end of the Iran-Iraq conflict in 1988, the Defense Ministry has been under the control of the IRGC, and its minister is always selected from the ranks of senior IRGC commanders.

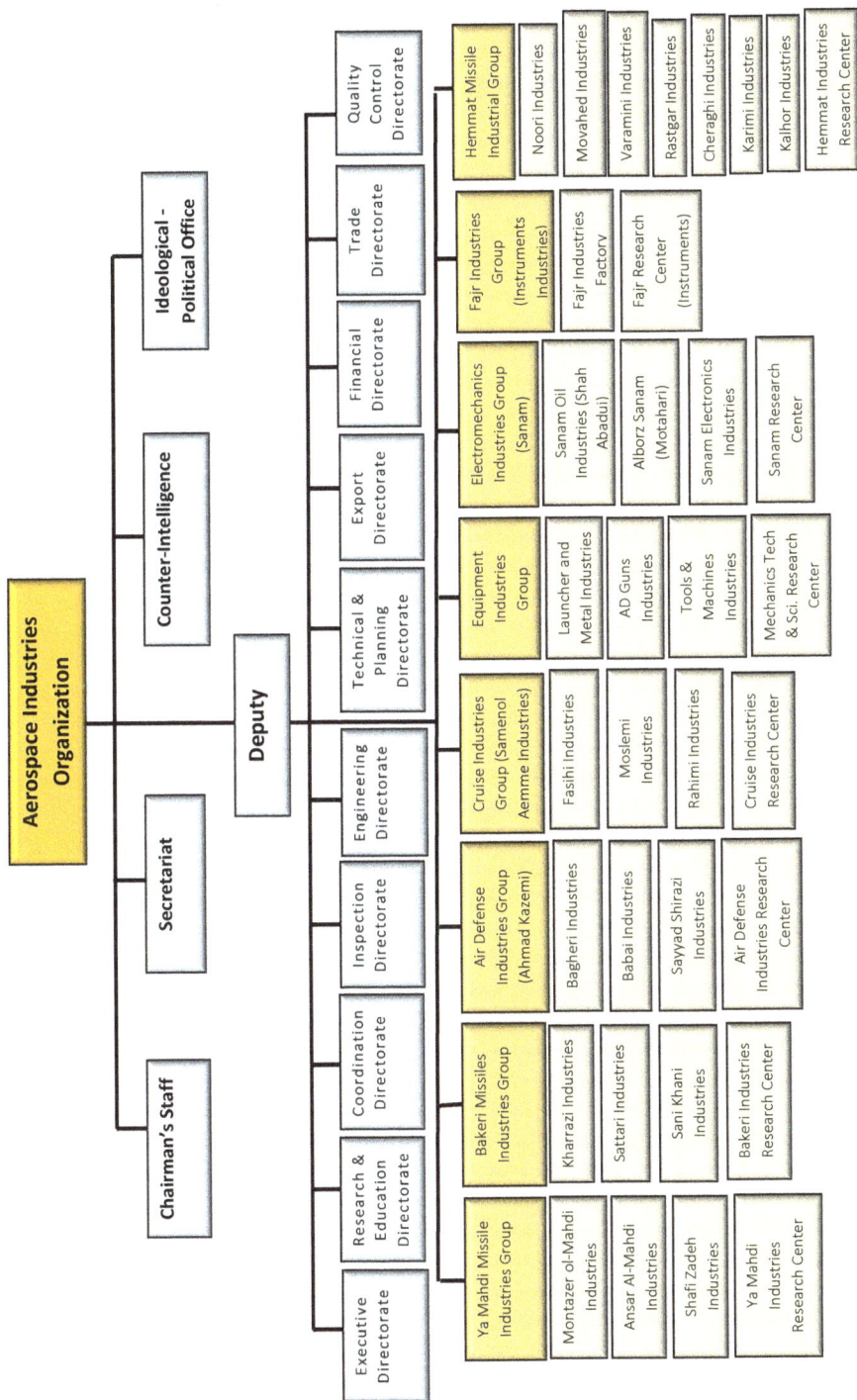

Aerospace Industries Organization

- Chairman's Staff
- Secretariat
- Counter-Intelligence
- Ideological - Political Office

Deputy

- Executive Directorate
- Research & Education Directorate
- Coordination Directorate
- Inspection Directorate
- Engineering Directorate
- Technical & Planning Directorate
- Export Directorate
- Financial Directorate
- Trade Directorate
- Quality Control Directorate

Ya Mahdi Missile Industries Group
- Montazer ol-Mahdi Industries
- Ansar Al-Mahdi Industries
- Shafi Zadeh Industries
- Ya Mahdi Industries Research Center

Bakeri Missiles Industries Group
- Kharrazi Industries
- Sattari Industries
- Sani Khani Industries
- Bakeri Industries Research Center

Air Defense Industries Group (Ahmad Kazemi)
- Bagheri Industries
- Babai Industries
- Sayyad Shirazi Industries
- Air Defense Industries Research Center

Cruise Industries Group (Samenol Aemme Industries)
- Fasihi Industries
- Moslemi Industries
- Rahimi Industries
- Cruise Industries Research Center

Equipment Industries Group
- Launcher and Metal Industries
- AD Guns Industries
- Tools & Machines Industries
- Mechanics Tech & Sci. Research Center

Electromechanics Industries Group (Sanam)
- Sanam Oil Industries (Shah Abadui)
- Alborz Sanam (Motahari)
- Sanam Electronics Industries
- Sanam Research Center

Fajr Industries Group (Instruments Industries)
- Fajr Industries Factory
- Fajr Research Center (Instruments)

Hemmat Missile Industrial Group
- Noori Industries
- Movahed Industries
- Varamini Industries
- Rastgar Industries
- Cheraghi Industries
- Karimi Industries
- Kalhor Industries
- Hemmat Industries Research Center

Hemmat Missile Industrial Group

The Hemmat Missile Industrial Group is the main unit responsible for the production of ballistic missiles such as Shahab 3, which runs on liquid fuel. As such, the group and its commanders and managers have been placed on UN sanctions lists.

The command center of the Hemmat Missile Industrial Group is located in the Hekmatieh district. Its address is: Tehran-no Avenue, Abali road, Lashgarak road junction.

Hemmat's production units are located in the Khojir district, in southeastern Tehran, on the south side of Damavand road. The bulk of the production of this group takes place in secret tunnels dug inside mountains. Even the administrative offices of the complex are built underground.

The Hemmat industrial group is comprised of the following departments, which due to their secret nature are identified by codenames:

- ☑ Kalhor industries, codename 1500, related to launch systems
- ☑ Karimi industries, codename 2500, related to fire chain
- ☑ Cheraghi industries, codename 3000, related to fuel production
- ☑ Rastgar industries, codename 4500, related to missile engine production
- ☑ Varamini industries, codename 6000, related to guidance and control systems production
- ☑ Movahed industries, codename 7500, related to shell and final assembly production
- ☑ Nouri industries, codename 8500, related to the production of warheads

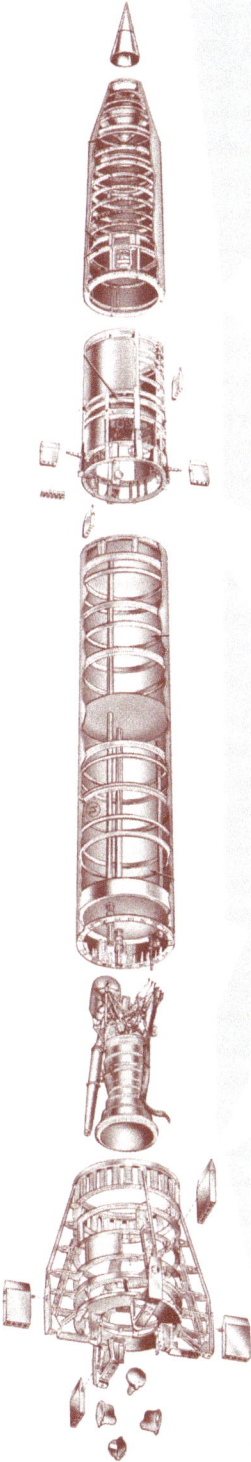

8500 NOURI INDUSTRIES
PRODUCTION OF WARHEADS

7500 MOVAHED INDUSTRIES
SHELL & FINAL ASSEMBLY

6000 VARAMINI INDUSTRIES
GUIDANCE & CONTROL SYSTEMS
PRODUCTION

4500 RASTGAR INDUSTRIES
MISSILE ENGINE PRODUCTION

3000 CHERAGHI INDUSTRIES
FUEL PRODUCTION

2500 KARIMI INDUSTRIES
FIRE CHAIN

1500 KALHOR INDUSTRIES
LAUNCH SYSTEMS

Bakeri Missile Industrial Group

The Bakeri Missile Industrial Group, a subsidiary of the AIO, is involved in manufacturing surface-to-surface missiles. This group primarily works on the production of liquid and solid fuel missiles and has been involved in the production of ballistic and Shahab missiles. Some of its manufacturing plants are located in the Khojir region, and it is comprised of four sub-groups named Kharrazi, Sani Khani, Sattari, and Eslami (Academy).

Ya Mahdi Missile Industrial Group

Headquartered in Shian-Lavizan, the Ya Mahdi Group acts as part of the regime's missile supply chain.[26] Portions of the technical parts of centrifuges and other equipment required by the regime's nuclear program are also produced in the group's manufacturing plants. One of its sites is located in the Abyek district north of the Karaj-Qazvin highway.

---

[26] Ya Mahdi Industries Group is an entity designated under OFAC's SDN Sanctions List for Weapons of Mass Destruction Proliferators Sanctions Regulations, 31 C.F.R. part 544 (NPWMD) and Iranian Financial Sanctions Regulations, 31 CFR part 561 (IFSR).

Iranian Regime's Missile Centers Across Iran Associated with AIO

NO	BASE CENTER	GOV. BODY	SUBJECT	LOCATION	TYPE OF ACTIVITY	NOTES
1	Aerospace Industries Organization Center	Defense Ministry	Command Post of Aerospace Industries Org.	Nobonyad Circle, North of Tehran	Production Command Post	Aerospace Industries Organization Main Office
2	Hemmat Missile Industries Command	Aerospace Organization	Command Post	North of Damavand Street	Production	Hemmat Industries Command Post, Former Accommodation, N. Korea Experts
3	Factory of Hemmat Missile Industries Group (Khojir Complex)	Aerospace Organization	Manufacturing Site for Ballistic Missiles (e.g. Shahab 3) and Solid Fuel Missiles	Khojir Region Southeast of Tehran	Production	Dozens of Factories Built in Underground Tunnels
4	Factory of Bakeri Missile Industries Group (Khojir Complex)	Aerospace Organization	Manufacturing Site for Ballistic Missiles and Solid Fuel Missiles	Khojir Region Southeast of Tehran	Production	Dozens of Factories Built in Underground Tunnels
5	Equipment Manufacturing Complex (Mahalati Industries)	Aerospace Organization	Manufacturing Site for Launching Pad of Ballistic Missiles and AA Guns	1 km on Telo Road, Azmayesh Junction, Damavand Street, Tehran	Production	Site for Making Missiles Launching Pad and Other Mechanical Parts of Missiles
6	Cruise Industries Group (Plan 4 Parchin Complex)	Aerospace Organization	Planning and Manufacturing Various Missiles	Northern Part of Parchin Complex, opposite Big Circle	Production	The Group Has Several Factories on the Site
7	Air Defense Industries Group (Plan 10 Parchin Complex)	Aerospace Organization	Planning and Manufacturing Various Missiles	Northern Part of Parchin Complex, South of Big Circle	Production	The Group Has Several Factories Partly in Parchin and other in Outskirts of Tehran
8	Other Missiles Industries (Plans 9 & 12 Parchin Complex)	Aerospace Organization	Missile Industries in Parchin	Parchin Complex, Garmsar Highway	Production	Other Missiles Industries Group Have Factories on This Site

NO	BASE CENTER	GOV. BODY	SUBJECT	LOCATION	TYPE OF ACTIVITY	NOTES
9	Shahabadi Industries	Aerospace Organization	Part of Sanam Industries, Metal Parts and Oil Drilling	Araj Junction, Pasdaran Street, Tehran	Production	This is Part of Sanam Group used for Purchasing Missiles Equipment
10	Bagheri Industries	Aerospace Organization	Part of Air Defense Industries	km 7, Old Tehran - Karaj Hway	Production	Factory Producing Part of Air Defense Equipment
11	Motahari Industries (Sanam Alborz)	Aerospace Organization	Part of Sanam, Equipment Manufacturing	Hekmat 12 Street, Qazvin industrial Complex	Production	Front Company for Producing Household Appliances But Part of Sanam Group
12	Ya Mahdi Missiles Industries Group	Aerospace Organization	Manufacturing Missile Parts and Centrifuges Parts	Adjacent to the Wood, Shian Street, Lavizan, Tehran	Production	The Site Runs Several Factories in Tehran and Karaj - Qazvin Highway
13	Part of Ya Mahdi Industries	Aerospace Organization	Missiles Parts Production Site	North of Abyek Highway, Qazvin	Production	Part of Ya Mahdi Industries Group Located inside Tunnels North of Abyek Highway
14	Shafizadeh Industry, Part of Ya Mahdi	Aerospace Organization	Producing Part of Missiles	Qazvin Industrial Complex	Production	This is Part of Ya Mahdi Industries
15	Haft-Tir Complex - Isfahan	IRGC Aerospace Industries	Missile Production and Arsenal	Close to Zarrin Shahr, South of Isfahan	Production	This Consists of Several Underground Tunnels Accommodating Nuclear and Missiles Activities as well as Making Ammunitions

Hemmat Industries Group

Hemmat Industries Group is the largest missile industry group and is responsible for producing the Shahab 3 and liquid fuel missiles.[27] Its command center and factories are located in the Khojir region of eastern Tehran.

Hemmat Industries Command Center

Khojir area in southwest Tehran - Hemmat Industries

---

[27] Hemmat Industries Group is an entity designated under OFAC's SDN Sanctions List for Weapons of Mass Destruction Proliferators Sanctions Regulations, 31 C.F.R. part 544 and Iranian Financial Sanctions Regulations, 31 CFR part 561.

The Bakeri Industries Group

The Bakeri Industries Group, which is involved in the production of solid fuel missiles, is located in the Khojir region.[28]

Bakeri Industries Group in Khojir

Parts Manufacturing Group (Mechanic)

The Parts Manufacturing Group (Mechanic) manufactures missile launch pads and other equipment related to the missiles industry. It is a part of Aerospace Industries Organization and is located north of the Damavand Street, 1 km on Telo Road, Azmayesh junction.[29]

The Parts Manufacturing Group near Hemmat Industries Command Center

---

[28] Shahid Bakeri Industrial Group is an entity designated under OFAC's SDN Sanctions List for Weapons of Mass Destruction Proliferators Sanctions Regulations, 31 C.F.R. part 544 (NPWMD) and Iranian Financial Sanctions Regulations, 31 CFR part 561 (IFSR).

[29] Aerospace Industries Organization is an entity designated under OFAC's SDN Sanctions List for Weapons of Mass Destruction Proliferators Sanctions Regulations, 31 C.F.R. part 544 (NPWMD) and Iranian Financial Sanctions Regulations, 31 CFR part 561 (IFSR).

Missile Sites in Parchin Military Complex

General Area of Parchin in Southwest Tehran

Plan 4 in Parchin

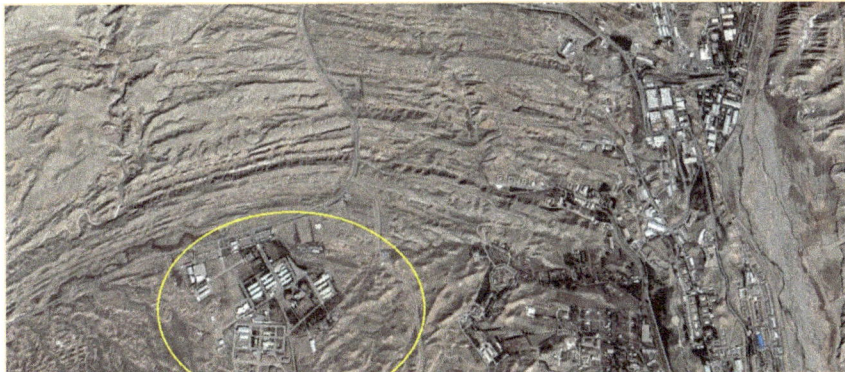

Plan 10 in Parchin

Shahabadi Industries (Araj)

Shahabadi Industries is a part of the Sanam Industries, a subsidiary of the Aerospace Industries Organization and is responsible for purchasing missiles equipment under this name.[30] It is located at Araj Junction, Pasdaran Street, Tehran.

Shahabadi Industries, located in Pasdaran Street purchases missile equipment

---

[30] Sanam Industries Group is an entity designated under OFAC's SDN Sanctions List for Weapons of Mass Destruction Proliferators Sanctions Regulations, 31 C.F.R. part 544 (NPWMD) and Iranian Financial Sanctions Regulations, 31 CFR part 561 (IFSR).

The Ya Mahdi Industries Group

Abyek area

Ya Mahdi-Abyek

Ya Mahdi-Shian

Missile Sites in Qazvin

36°10'13"N 50°5'29"E

Shafizadeh Industries Missile Site

36°10'23"N 50°5'29"E

Motahari Industries Missile Site

Haft-Tir Complex — Isfahan

Haft-Tir Complex, is close to Zarrin Shahr, south of Isfahan. The site consists of several underground tunnels accommodating nuclear and missiles activities as well as manufacturing ammunitions.

Haft-Tir Complex near Isfahan consists of several underground tunnels

4

Construction of Tunnels and Underground Structures

On the basis of conclusions gleaned from the country's defeat in the Iran-Iraq war, the regime began digging tunnels and building underground facilities for sensitive military and security initiatives. The plan, called Passive Defense, stresses the pursuit of nuclear weapons and ballistic missiles. Some of the most senior IRGC commanders have pursued this project since the Iran-Iraq ceasefire in 1988.[31]

Supreme Leader, Ali Khamenei.

Hassan Firouzabadi, member of the Expediency Discernment Council and senior military advisor to Ali Khamenei

In 1989, on the orders of the regime's new Supreme Leader Ali Khamenei,[32] IRGC veteran Hassan Firouzabadi[33], then-Deputy Chief of Staff of the Armed Forces, was assigned to implement the plans. It was decided that all of the regime's

[31] "Passive Defense Organization," *Iran Watch*, November 1, 2010, https://www.iranwatch.org/iranian-entities/passive-defense-organization.

[32] Vasudevan Sridharan, "Iran Searching for Ayatollah Khamenei's successor amid concerns over leader's health," *IBT,* December 14, 2015, https://www.ibtimes.co.uk/iran-searching-ayatollah-khameneis-successor-amid-concerns-over-leaders-health-1533193.

[33] "Top Iranian General Urges Muslims to Refuse Saudi 'Anti-Terrorism' Coalition," *ABNA*, December 20, 2015, http://en.abna24.com/service/iran/archive/2015/12/20/725954/story.html.

sensitive military sites, nuclear-related facilities, and missile-related facilities should be relocated to underground sites or to sites built inside mountains. The regime set up underground command centers for emergency situations and established centers for the preservation of the production and manufacturing of assault weapons, missiles, and other elements of the nuclear program.

AGENCIES AND ENTITIES ENGAGED

In order to implement the Passive Defense plan, the regime has used many of its military organs especially the Khatam al-Anbia construction company and the Defense Ministry. The IRGC's engineering units divided the country into particular zones and began implementing the above-mentioned projects. The names and details of some of the main companies involved in building tunnels and secret military facilities are:

1. Khatam al-Anbia Construction Headquarters is the primary oversight body for all IRGC and other military engineering units.[34] Khatam is also active in extensive commercial activities and plundering of Iran's national wealth. It has set up giant subsidiaries and other companies, some of which have international connections.[35]

2. The executive management unit for construction projects related to the aerospace organization in the Defense Ministry is involved in building the tunnels and manufacturing concrete for the regime's nuclear

---

[34] Khatam al-Anbia Construction (Khatam Al Anbia Gharargah Sazandegi Nooh) is an entity designated under OFAC's SDN Sanctions List for Weapons of Mass Destruction Proliferators Sanctions Regulations, 31 C.F.R. part 544 (NPWMD), Iranian Financial Sanctions Regulations, 31 CFR part 561 (IFSR), Iranian Financial Sanctions Regulations, 31 CFR Part 561 (IRGC), and Global Terrorism Sanctions Regulations, 31 C.F.R. part 594 (SDGT)

[35] "Iran; The Rise of The Revolutionary Guard's Financial Empire," NCRI-US, March 2017.

and missiles initiatives. Its headquarters is in the Khojir region and has an office located at Tehran's Khorshid Avenue.

3. Pars Garma Construction and Industrial Organization is active in building tunnels and facilities, including some at Parchin and Khojir. The company has also been active in the Khojir 1 and Khojir 2 projects. Its office is located near the end of Teymouri Street, Langari Avenue, Nobonyad Square, Tehran.

4. Pars Banay-e Sabz Construction and Industrial Company is located within the defense industries organization and is active in the fields of building tunnels, manufacturing missile launch pads, building airport facilities, installing machinery, building concrete structures, passive defense facilities, and ammunition bunkers, among others. Some of the tunnels at Parchin, Khojir and Isfahan's Haft-e Tir have been built by this company.

5. Parsian Technology Company operated under the name of Defense Industries Consulting Engineers for some time. However, it later changed its name to Mosharsad and then to Parsian. The company is involved in building military structures and was active in the Khojir 1 and Khojir 2 projects. The Defense Ministry continues to change the names of its affiliate companies in order to maintain secrecy.

6. Hara Institute is tied to the terrorist Qods Force (extraterritorial arm of the IRGC).[36] It receives orders

---

[36] Hara Institute, also known as "Hara Company," is an entity designated under OFAC's SDN Sanctions List for Weapons of Mass Destruction Proliferators Sanctions Regulations, 31 C.F.R. part 544 (NPWMD), Iranian Financial Sanctions Regulations, 31 CFR part 561 (IFSR), Iranian Financial Sanctions Regulations, 31 CFR Part 561 (IRGC), and Global Terrorism Sanctions Regulations, 31 C.F.R. part 594 (SDGT), https://sanctionssearch.ofac.treas.gov/Details.aspx?id=1802

and requests from Khatam Construction and has close relations with Qorb Nouh (the IRGC navy's engineering arm). This organization has executed many of the IRGC's naval projects. Ehtesam, the head of the institution, is a former IRGC member. Ehtesam. The manager of the organizations defense designs is an engineer named Alizadeh and the head of its technical unit is an engineer named Karimi.

7. Qorb-e Qaem is involved in some of the projects to build secret structures and tunnels. The head office of the company is located directly across from the Vali Asr Garrison (formerly Eshrat Abad) in Tehran. Its commander is an IRGC veteran named Nouri.

8. Iran Tunnel Association is a non-military, commercial company. In addition to the military organs operating to advance the above-mentioned designs, the regime also uses the cover and resources of such non-military companies. The Iran Tunnel Association, founded by former president Mahmoud Ahmadinejad in 1998, has been used to obtain new scientific designs and information from other countries and transfer them to Iran in order to then be used for military projects.

5

Nuclear-Ballistic Nexus

NUCLEAR COOPERATION BETWEEN AEROSPACE INDUSTRIES ORGANIZATION AND SPND

The design and production of nuclear warheads has been one of the most controversial aspects of the Iranian regime's nuclear program. As stated prior, the regime is pursuing a strategy of deterrence. This strategy requires that a country capable of manufacturing nuclear weapons be able to design and apply related technology to a missile as a delivery method or have an effective and safe airplane to relocate the nuclear weapon, or a sufficiently protected naval vessel to move the nuclear weapon. Since the Iranian regime lacks suitable planes or submarines with which to display its deterrent force, it has organized its resources to advance ballistic missile systems as a delivery method for nuclear weapons.

The Hemmat Industrial Group, which is the most important component of the Aerospace Industries Organization, conducts the design and production of nuclear warheads. The Hemmat group is responsible for the production of Shahab 1, 2, 3 and Qadr missiles. One of the manufacturing factories used for the development of a nuclear warhead is the Alireza Nouri group and is identified by codename 8500.

Developing nuclear warheads

The Organization of Defensive Innovation and Research, known by its Farsi acronym SPND, is the regime's organ for developing nuclear weapons. One of its subdivisions is the Center for Aerospace Research and New Technological Designs (*markaze tahghighat va tarahie fanavarihaye novine hava va faza*). This division works on the designs and electronic calculations required for a nuclear warhead. Its current head is Dr. Erfan Bali Lashak. Previously, he was the chair of the Malek Ashtar Electronics Complex. Dr. Kamran Daneshjoo, former Minister of Science in Ahmadinejad's cabinet, was the head of the center from 2002 to 2005. Numerous documents in the hands of the International Atomic Energy Agency (IAEA) carry the signature of Dr. Daneshjoo.

IAEA reports

IAEA reports contain studies and evidence of extensive efforts indicative of the Iranian regime's intent to acquire a nuclear warhead. In an attachment to its May 2008 report, the IAEA published documents related to the design of a missile warhead, naming design of a missile warhead, naming Mohsen Fakhrizadeh as head of the project with oversight on Project 111.[37] The IAEA also has documents with respect to the Center for Aerospace Research and New Technological Designs, referred to as the E6 Group. For example, in the May 2008 IAEA report, "Document 8: 'Instructions for Assembling the Chamber Parts, Assembling the Payload Inside the Chamber, and Assembling the Chamber to Shahab-3 Warhead', 18 pages

---

[37] IAEA Inspector General "Implementation of the NPT Safeguards Agreement and Relevant Provisions of Security Council resolutions 1737 (2006), 1747 (2007), and 1803 (2008), in the Islamic Republic of Iran," IAEA, May 26, 2008, https://www.iaea.org/sites/default/files/gov2008-15.pdf.

in Farsi, dated December 2003–January 2004, produced by Group E6 of Project 111."[38] In the Appendix to the November 2011 IAEA report, the agency also produces evidence of the Iranian regime's work on nuclear warheads, including designs.[39]

The Tinner Case

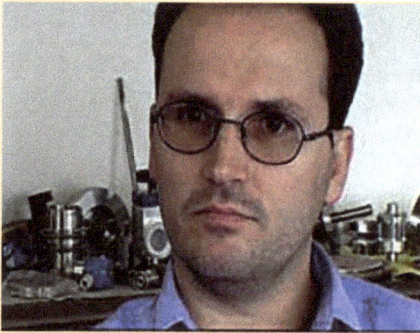

Urs Tinner supplied centrifuge parts and participated in smuggling ring along with father, Friedrich Tinner and brother, Marco Tinner.

In 2004, the Swiss police arrested three Swiss citizens and confiscated a computer containing extremely sensitive information belonging to them.[40] Friedrich Tinner and his two sons, Urs and Marco, were among the engineers and experts producing and smuggling centrifuges and nuclear warheads.[41,42] The information stored on their

---

[38] Ibid.

[39] IAEA Inspector General, "Implementation of the NPT Safeguards Agreement and Relevant Provisions of Security Council resolutions 1737 (2006), 1747 (2007), and 1803 (2008), in the Islamic Republic of Iran," *IAEA*, November 8, 2011, http://ncrius.org/wp-content/uploads/2016/04/IAEA_Iran_8Nov2011.pdf.

[40] David Albright and Paul Brannan, "The Tinner Case: Time for a Frank, Open Evaluation," *Institute for Science and International Security,* December 21, 2010, isis-online.org/uploads/isis-reports/documents/tinner_case_evaluation_21Dec2010.pdf.

[41] Behrouz Mehri, "Nuclear smugglers who aided AQ Khan face trial in Switzerland," Getty Images, *The Guardian*, https://www.theguardian.com/world/2011/dec/13/nuclear-smugglers-aq-khan-switzerland

[42] Joseph Fitsanakis, "Nuclear smugglers to get reduced prison sentences 'for helping CIA'," *Intel News,* September 9, 2012, https://intelnews.org/tag/tinner-nuclear-smuggling-ring/.

hard drive included blueprints for a sophisticated nuclear warhead, and revealed that the Tinners worked for the A.Q. Khan network. The network is headed by the Pakistani scientist Abdul Qadeer (A.Q.) Khan, a nuclear hero that turned into a black marketeer. A.Q. Khan was responsible for legally developing Pakistan's nuclear arsenal and sent shockwaves across the world when he confessed on live television to illegally proliferating nuclear weapons to Iran, Libya, and North Korea.[43] In a Spring 2008 article, David Albright, a former UN weapons inspector and head of the Institute for Science and International Security, highlighted the role of the Tinners in transmitting sensitive information to Iran.

Albright said the "construction plans" included previously undisclosed designs for a compact warhead that could fit on Iran's medium-range ballistic missiles," and that, "they [Iran and North Korea] both faced struggles in building a nuclear warhead small enough to fit atop their ballistic missiles, and these designs were for a warhead that would fit."[44]

Citing information provided by IAEA investigators, Albright contended that the blueprint found on the computer of Friedrich Tinner and his sons resembles the warhead blueprint that Pakistan has in its nuclear arsenal. Linking the Tinners to the Khan network, he said that, "Khan may have transferred his own country's most secret and dangerous information to foreign smugglers so that they could sell it for a profit."[45]

---

[43] Catherine Collins and Douglas Frantz, "The Long Shadow of A.Q. Khan," *Foreign Affairs,* January 31, 2018 https://www.foreignaffairs.com/articles/north-korea/2018-01-31/long-shadow-aq-khan

[44] Ian Traynor, "Blueprint for Nuclear Warhead Found on Smugglers' Computers," The Guardian, June 15, 2008, https://www.theguardian.com/world/2008/jun/16/nuclear.pakistan

[45] Joby Warrick, "Smugglers Had Design For Advanced Warhead," *The Washington Post,* June 15, 2008, http://www.washingtonpost.com/wp-dyn/content/article/2008/06/14/AR2008061402032.html

The documents found on the Tinners' computer indicate that the size of the nuclear bomb was smaller and more advanced than earlier versions. It could easily fit on long-range ballistic missile warheads. The source of the design for a nuclear bomb by the Iranian regime, which was also referenced in studies and reports made public on the Iranian nuclear program by former IAEA director general Mohamed ElBaradei, was found in the Tinner house in Switzerland.[46]

---

[46] "Briefing Notes from February 2008 IAEA Meeting Regarding Iran's Nuclear Program," The Institute for Science and International Security (ISIS), April 11, 2008, http://ncrius.org/wp-content/uploads/2016/04/IAEA_Briefing_Weaponization.pdf

UNINSPECTED SITES

The Iranian regime and IRGC run a multitude of nuclear sites that have gone uninspected by the IAEA despite the demands by the international community. The International Atomic Energy Agency (IAEA) has both an obligation and a legal authority to inspect these locations. Past IAEA reports, have documented a long list of unanswered questions about the Iranian regime's ongoing effort to acquire a nuclear warhead.[47]

On April 4, 2018, former Deputy Director-General of the IAEA and head of IAEA Department of Safeguards Olli Heinonen published a report outlining the need for the IAEA to inspect all suspect sites including the military facilities in Iran. The military, he says, has played a key role in developing Iran's nuclear program, which means that their sites must be inspected in order to effectively monitor the Iranian regime's nuclear activities. Importantly, Heinonen emphasizes that "Iran cannot declare any site to be a sanctuary off-limits to IAEA inspectors" due to the requirements of the Nuclear Nonproliferation Treaty, among other agreements. In addition, Heinonen writes in the report, "Iran actually agreed to IAEA monitoring" of these facilities.

Six main uninspected sites have been identified by the Iranian resistance as being involved in the nuclear weapons project of the regime.[48]

---

[47] IAEA Inspector General, "Implementation of the NPT Safeguards Agreement and Relevant Provisions of Security Council resolutions 1737 (2006), 1747 (2007), and 1803 (2008), in the Islamic Republic of Iran," *IAEA*, November 8, 2011, http://ncrius.org/wp-content/uploads/2016/04/IAEA_Iran_8Nov2011.pdf.

[48] Iran's Nuclear Core," published by *NCRI-US*, October 10, 2017, http://www.ncrius.org/irannuclearcore.html

1. Pazhouheshkadeh

One of the 7 subdivisions of SPND, the unit responsible for conducting research and building a trigger for a nuclear weapon is known by its Farsi acronym METFAZ. The April 2017 revelation of NCRI showed that METFAZ has transferred its main activities to plan 6 at the Parchin military complex in southeast Tehran, known as Pazhouheshkadeh (Research Academy).

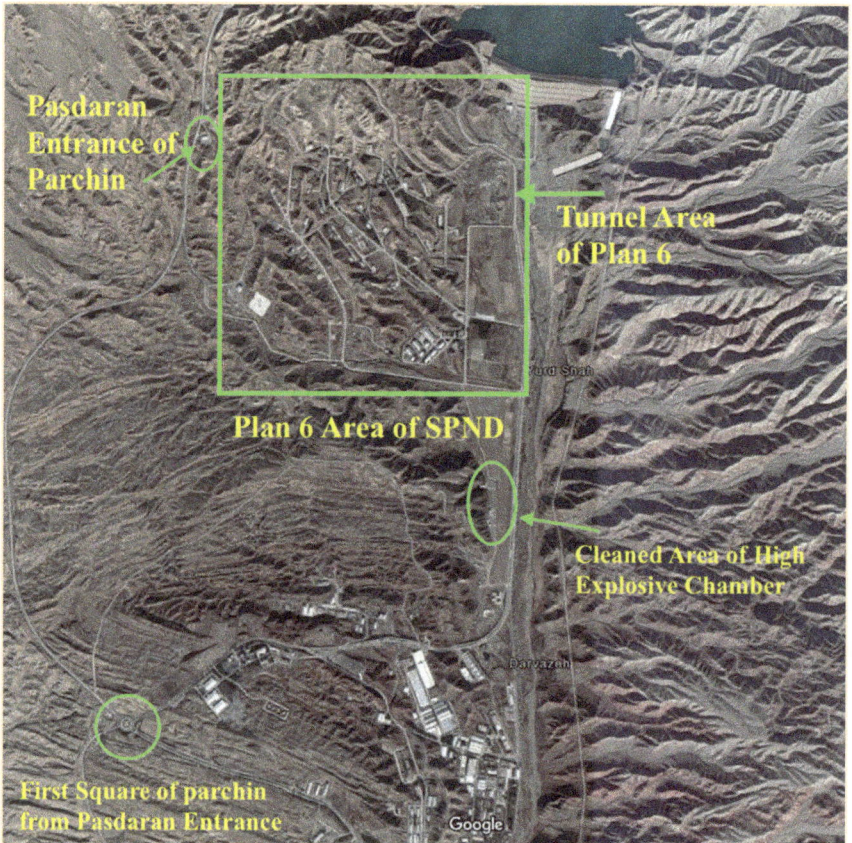

Plan 6, Pazhouheshkadeh, at Parchin military complex where SPND has been conducting tests

2. Nouri Industry Site

The project conducted at this site, located in Khojir area southeast of Tehran is overseen by SPND. Due to the sensitivity of the nuclear program and manufacturing of warheads, the Nouri Industry site has its own security and a large underground tunnel program. The warheads in this location are designed for installation on Shahab 3 missiles. North Korean officials cooperate substantially with regime experts in this project.

Nouri Industries involved in developing nuclear warhead

3. Hafte Tir site

The Hafte Tir site belongs to the Defense Ministry and is located in a military zone near the city of Isfahan in a mountainous area; it was constructed under the supervision of SPND. The nuclear research site within Hafte Tir is located in a nearly half-mile-long tunnel.

Hafte Tir Military Industrial Complex under the supervision of SPND

4. Sanjarian site

This site used to be the main testing site for METFAZ, one of the subdivisions of SPND focused on explosives and trigger mechanisms for nuclear weapons. This site is east of Tehran, on the banks of the Jajrood River.

SPND's METFAZ site near Sanjarian village

5. Mojdeh site

Mojdeh was the original venue of SPND's headquarters, and includes some research and workshops of a civilian nature."

SPND's Mojdeh side, the former location for the Headquarters

6. Nour building

This is the new headquarters of the SPND. It is affiliated with the Defense Ministry and is secured by air defense as well as full surveillance.

Nour Building, the new headquarter for SPND

6

Cooperation with North Korea

The Iranian regime is North Korea's strategic ally. Many of the regime's officials, including Khamenei, current President Hassan Rouhani, and Mohsen Rezai[49], the former Commander-in-chief of the IRGC, have all traveled to North Korea to discuss the nuclear program.[50]

Former Commander-in-chief of the IRGC, Mohsen Rezai, has travelled to North Korea

According to reports by the regime's Foreign Ministry, the Iranian ambassador to North Korea has a ceremonial role whereas the main points of contact with North Korea are the most senior commanders of the IRGC. According to these reports, the regime's Foreign Ministry and its ambassadors are not briefed on the direct negotiations between the IRGC and the Defense Ministry with the North Korean armed forces. In exchange for obtaining military, nuclear and missile equipment and resources, the Iranian regime sends oil to North Korea. These deals are not within the purview of Tehran's Foreign Ministry.

Missile and nuclear experts from North Korea have had a consistent presence in Iran since the Iran-Iraq War. In 2015,

---

[49] "Erbil-Based Operation Room behind Recent Unrest in Iran," Iran Front Page, January 17, 2018, http://ifpnews.com/exclusive/erbil-based-operation-room-behind-recent-unrest-in-iran/.

[50] Guy Taylor, "Iranian-North Korean Talks Raise Specter of Cooperation on Military, Ballistic Missile Technology," The Washington Times, November 28, 2017, www.washingtontimes.com/news/2017/nov/28/fresh-concern-over-possible-iran-north-korea-nucle/.

a nuclear delegation from North Korea, composed of seven experts, spent the last week of April in Iran.[51] This was the third such nuclear and missile delegation to visit Iran from North Korea in 2015.

The delegates included nuclear experts, nuclear warhead experts, and experts in various areas of ballistic missiles, including guidance systems. The North Korean delegations have also provided assistance and consultation in the areas of aerodynamics, missile body design, and electronic components of warheads.

Secretive transit and lodging for North Korean experts

Due to the highly sensitive nature of these activities, the nuclear and missile delegations from North Korea enter and leave Iran in total secrecy. They stay in the special guesthouse of the Aerospace Industries Organization (AIO) near the Hemmat Industrial Group site in the Khojir area, located in eastern Tehran.

The AIO has designated a protected site to accommodate foreign experts. This location is in the Hakimiyeh area in the eastern part of Tehran Province. Known as the Imam Khomeini Complex, also known as 2000 units, this site is controlled by the Ministry of Defense and is also used by its personnel.

The specific guesthouse is located in block 1, Koye Yas, number 5, of the Imam Khomeini Complex. It is an eight-story building at the back, is separated from other sections by a fence, and is camouflaged.

---

[51] John Irish, "North Korean nuclear, missile experts visit Iran-dissidents," *Reuters,* May 28, 2015, https://www.reuters.com/article/us-iran-northkorea-dissidents/north-korean-nuclear-missile-experts-visit-iran-dissidents-idUSKBN0OD08F20150528.

The satellite imagery of the Imam Khomeini Complex and Hemmat Industries Complex

The exact location of the place where North Koreans stay is: End of Babaie Highway heading to the east, past Morvarid Hall, at Khomeini complex.

The venue is adjacent to the factories of Hemmat Industries, and the North Korean experts enter the Hemmat site via a special route from the guest house and proceed to Hemmat and Bakeri Missile Industries at the south of Damavand road in the Khojir area. The North Korean experts are moved in vans with tinted windows and curtains. The counterintelligence department of the Ministry of Defense controls the guesthouse under tight security.

Fakhrizadeh and SPND experts at a North Korean nuclear test

According to compiled reports, delegations of experts and commanders of the IRGC and Ministry of Defense, particularly those working in the nuclear and missile-related fields, visit North Korea regularly. According to reliable intelligence, Mohsen Fakhrizadeh was present during the third nuclear test conducted by North Korea on February 12, 2013.

Mohsen Fakhrizadeh, travelled to North Korea to observe its third nuclear test.

After a two-year investigation, the Iranian Resistance established that Fakhrizadeh travelled to North Korea through China under the alias of Dr. Hassan Mohseni. During the visit, Fakhrizadeh stayed at Hotel Koryo in Pyongyang, which is considered to be the second most luxurious hotel in the city. Two other nuclear experts from SPND accompanied Fakhrizadeh during the North Korean nuclear test visit. Mansour Chavoshi, the Iranian regime's Ambassador to North Korea, personally welcomed Fakhrizadeh and facilitated his communications and exchanges with North Korean officials.

Fakhrizadeh stayed at Hotel Koryo in Pyongyang, North Korea

Fakhrizadeh spent only two hours in the Iranian regime's embassy in Pyongyang and made no other visits to the embassy during this trip. In order to keep Fakhrizadeh's real identity a secret, he was referred to by the alias Dr. Mohseni. The trip was coordinated between the Iranian and North Korean ministries of defense, with the Iranian side paying for all expenses.

The Iranian regime's embassy in Pyongyang, North Korea

7

Tehran's Violations and International Response

The IRGC's missile programs have been sanctioned by the UN Security Council because they threaten regional countries as well as peace and security. Organizations, companies and individuals related to the missile program have been placed under sanctions in multiple UN Security Council resolutions dating from 2006 to 2010.[52]

Article 9 of UN Security Council Resolution 1929 states: "Decides that Iran shall not undertake any activity related to ballistic missiles capable of delivering nuclear weapons, including launches using ballistic missile technology, and that States shall take all necessary measures to prevent the transfer of technology or technical assistance to Iran related to such activities."[53]

Following the nuclear deal with the Iranian regime, formally known as the Joint Plan of Comprehensive Action (JCPOA) signed in July 2015, all previous UN Security Council resolutions with respect to the regime's missile program were rescinded and replaced by Resolution 2231. Adopted after the nuclear deal, Resolution 2231 lists restrictions on the regime's missile industry in Annex B while invoking Chapter 7 of the UN Charter.[54]

In Article 3 of Annex B, Iran is called upon not to undertake any activity related to ballistic missiles designed to be capable of delivering nuclear weapons, including launches using such

---

[52] United Nations Security Council resolutions 1737 (2006), 1803 (2008), and 1929 (2010).

[53] "S/RES/1929 (2010) Security Council Subsidiary Organs," *United Nations Security Council*, June 9, 2010, https://www.un.org/sc/suborg/en/s/res/1929-(2010).

[54] United Nations Security Council Resolution 2231, S/RES/2231, 20 July 2015, *United Nations Security Council,* http://www.securitycouncilreport.org/atf/cf/%7B65BFCF9B-6D27-4E9C-8CD3-CF6E4FF96FF9%7D/s_res_2231.pdf.

ballistic missile technology, until the date eight years after the JCPOA Adoption Day or until the date on which the IAEA submits a report confirming the Broader Conclusion, whichever is earlier.[55]

Article 4 of the Annex also states that for eight years, except if the Security Council decides in advance on a case-by-case basis, the Iranian regime is banned from purchase or transfer of materials, equipment, goods and technology that could be used in its missile industry.[56]

---

[55] Ibid.

[56] Ibid.

REGIONAL INVOLVEMENT AND EXPORT OF MISSILE TECHNOLOGY

One of the regime's measures in line with its objective of warmongering in the region is to create missile factories in various countries of the Middle East. The former Iranian ambassador to Syria, Hossein Sheikh ol-Eslam, said in November 2016: "Since the transfer of a large quantity of missile parts and equipment cannot be done, in order to create a missile industry in territories around Iran, we have tried to make sure that this can be done in those countries themselves to the extent possible."[57]

On November 11, 2014, the commander of the IRGC Aerospace, Amir Ali Hajizadeh, said, "thank God, our situation has improved today. Even the countries that helped us in those days [Iran-Iraq war], like Syria, later purchased missiles from us and now the factories for producing missiles in Syria are set up by Iran, and they produce missiles there designed by Iran."[58]

---

[57] "Our missile production units are not limited to the Syrian territory," *Entekhab News*, November 12, 2017, http://www.entekhab.ir/fa/news/304128

[58] "Commander: Syrian Missile-Manufacturing Plants Built by Iran," *Fars News,* November 11, 2014, http://en.farsnews.com/newstext. aspx?nn=13930820000325; "Commander Hajizadeh: Missile Factories of Syria Are Built by Iran/Supreme Leader Said the Missiles Should Have Precision Targeting," *Fars News*, November 11, 2014, http://www.farsnews. com/newstext.php?nn=13930806000232.

IRGC veteran and Major General Mohammad Baqeri[59], the head of the Armed Forces Chiefs of Staff, said on November 10, 2016: "Syria has reached a point where in recent years, Iran has set up a missile industry for it in Aleppo, where they are producing missiles."[60] Four days later, Hajizadeh, the commander of IRGC Aerospace, announced that the missile factories in Aleppo had been completely destroyed in the course of the conflict.[61]

Mohammad Baqeri, Major General and head of the Armed Forces Chiefs of Staff said Iran has set up a missile industry in Aleppo

During a Sky News interview on March 28, 2017, Arab military analyst, Riaz Kahvegi, discussed the creation of missile factories by the Iranian regime for the Lebanese Hezbollah.

"The Iranian regime had exported this technology in the past to Sudan. At the time, Sudan was an ally of the regime. Sudan manufactured Katyusha rockets for Hamas in Gaza and sent them to Gaza. ... Both before the Syrian revolution and

---

[59] "Iran to Withdraw from JCPOA If Sanctions Reinstated: Top General," *Iran Front Page*, October 30, 2017, http://ifpnews.com/exclusive/iran-withdraw-jcpoa-sanctions-reinstated-top-general/.

[60] "Iran in Violation of Security Council Resolution 2231 on Khamenei's Orders," *Iran Focus*, November 18, 2016, http://iranfocus.com/en/index.php?option=com_content&view=article&id=30982:iran-in-violation-of-security-council-resolution-2231-on-khamenei-s-orders&catid=9:terrorism&Itemid=114.

[61] Ibid.

after it, Iran sent missile technology to the Syrian regime. Currently, the situation in Syria is primarily managed by Russia, which has specific interests in Syria. The Iranian regime is afraid that Russia will strike a deal with Assad to prevent further cooperation with it. For Tehran, Syria acts as a bridge to send supplies to Hezbollah. Therefore, for the regime it is only logical to provide the resources to Hezbollah to build its own missiles, munitions and military equipment. This is done both in Lebanon and also in Hezbollah-controlled border regions in Syria."

On March 17, 2017, Iranian-made missiles killed at least 26 forces loyal to Yemen's government at a base east of Sana'a. A military official said that the Houthi militias used Iranian-made Zelzal missiles to target the mosque at the base.[62]

U.S. naval forces have been particularly prone to Iranian-made missile attacks by the Houthi rebels. According to Al-Jazeera, on October 16, 2016, U.S. naval officials reported four offensive Houthi missile attacks against the USS Mason in a span of just one week. On October 13, 2016, after coming under rocket fire by the Houthi forces twice in four days, the US Navy warships launched five Tomahawk cruise missiles at Houthi-controlled territories along Yemen's Red Sea coast. These defensive measures marked the first time the US has taken direct action against the rebel group.[63]

In 2018, Houthi rebels heightened rocket attacks against the Arab coalition. On March 25, 2018, Human Rights Watch reported that the Houthi rebels violated the laws of war

---

[62] "26 Yemen soldiers killed in Houthi missile attack," *Arab News,* March 18, 2017, http://www.arabnews.com/node/1070126/middle-east

[63] "Yemen war: US ship faces new round of 'Houthi missiles,'" *Al-Jazeera,* October 16, 2016, https://www.aljazeera.com/news/2016/10/yemen-war-ship-faces-houthi-missiles-161016034018318.html

by launching missiles at civilian populated areas in Saudi Arabia.[64] A spokesperson for the Saudi-led coalition, Colonel Turki al-Maliki, confirmed that one civilian was killed due to shrapnel as a result of the missile attacks, marking the first death in Riyadh since the start of the military campaign launched three years ago in Yemen.[65]

---

[64] "Saudi Arabia/Yemen: Houthi Missile Attacks Unlawful," *Human Rights Watch,* April 2, 2018, https://www.hrw.org/news/2018/04/02/saudi-arabia/yemen-houthi-missile-attacks-unlawful

[65] "Saudi Arabia: Houthi missile attack kills Egyptian in Riyadh," *Al-Jazeera,* March 26, 2018, https://www.aljazeera.com/news/2018/03/yemen-houthi-rebels-fire-ballistic-missile-riyadh-180325211734660.htm

SANCTIONS VIOLATIONS AND SMUGGLING METHODS

The regime and IRGC have established an extensive network to smuggle weapons and missile parts. Some of these activities have been consistently exposed by various countries and international media outlets. On August 19, 2010, German federal prosecutors said they had charged two men, identified as Mohsen Afrasiabi, and German businessman Heinz Ulrich K., for "buying from a German firm a furnace used in making warheads and missile guidance systems heat resistant."[66]

According to Reuters, a dual citizen of Iran and the United States was found guilty on November 22, 2016, on charges that he tried to help acquire surface-to-air missiles and aircraft components for the Iranian regime in violation of U.S. sanctions. "Reza Olangian was convicted by a federal jury in Manhattan on all four counts he faced, including conspiring to acquire and transfer anti-aircraft missiles, prosecutors said."[67]

The report goes on to say, "Olangian faces a mandatory minimum prison sentence of 25 years and a maximum of life. Olangian, who became a U.S. citizen in 1999, was arrested in

---

[66] "Germany Charges Two over Iran Exports," *The Sydney Morning Herald-World*, August 19, 2010, https://www.smh.com.au/world/germany-charges-two-over-iran-exports-20100819-12s0i.html.

[67] Nate Raymond, "U.S.-Iranian citizen convicted in U.S. for trying to buy missiles for Iran," *Reuters*, November 22, 2016, https://www.reuters.com/article/us-usa-iran-crime/u-s-iranian-citizen-convicted-in-u-s-for-trying-to-buy-missiles-for-iran-idUSKBN13I00R.

Estonia in October 2012 and subsequently extradited to the United States following a sting operation orchestrated by the U.S. Drug Enforcement Administration (DEA). Prosecutors said that in 2012, Olangian met in Ukraine with a DEA informant posing as a Russian weapons broker to arrange for the purchase of surface-to-air missiles and various military aircraft components. In recorded conversations and emails, Olangian described his plans to acquire the missiles and parts and smuggle them into Iran, for whose government he was purchasing them, from Afghanistan or from another neighboring country, prosecutors said. Prosecutors said Olangian negotiated a deal involving 10 missiles and dozens of aircraft parts, and during a video conference with the informant, stated that he ultimately wanted to acquire at least 200 missiles. The deal followed a failed effort by Olangian in 2007 to obtain about 100 missiles for Iran, prosecutors said. His goal throughout, they said, was to make a substantial profit selling the weapons."[68] On March 14, 2018, a U.S. District Judge in Manhattan sentenced Olangian to 25 years in prison.[69]

Evading sanctions

An April 2018 report in the Washington Post exposed the fact that the Iranian regime has been avoiding international sanctions, placed on them as a result of these nefarious activities, for over ten years. The report reveals "a multibillion-dollar corruption

---

[68] Nate Raymond, "U.S.-Iranian Citizen Convicted in U.S. for Trying to Buy Missiles," *Reuters*, November 23, 2016, https://www.reuters.com/article/us-usa-iran-crime/u-s-iranian-citizen-convicted-in-u-s-for-trying-to-buy-missiles-for-iran-idUSKBN13I00R.

[69] Brendan Pierson, "U.S.-Iranian man gets 25 years prison for trying to buy missiles for Iran," *Reuters*, March 14, 2018, https://www.reuters.com/article/us-usa-iran-crime/u-s-iranian-man-gets-25-years-prison-for-trying-to-buy-missiles-for-iran-idUSKCN1GQ2WV

scheme by a Persian Gulf bank that secretly helped Iran evade sanctions for more than a decade" by altering financial documents to mask a large amount of "illicit trade." The banks concealed more than $7 billion in transactions between 2004 and 2015, and the report also uncovers bank accounts tied to convicted IRGC officials and front companies. Based in Bahrain, the bank has been likened to a Trojan horse and has been "allowing Iran to buy and sell billions of dollars' worth of goods in defiance of international sanctions intended to punish Tehran over its nuclear program and support for terrorist groups."[70]

In another incident, four days into 2018, two Iranian nationals tried to buy parts of an advanced missile in Kyiv, according to a spokesperson for the Ukrainian intelligence service. This effort appears to have violated a UN arms embargo on Iran. Masked men in Ukraine's secret police arrested the men and found parts of the missile in their vehicle.[71]

Front companies

The Aerospace Industries Organization (AIO) generally uses commercial activities as a front for its operations to smuggle material into Iran.

Sanam Industrial Group

To cover up its military operations, the Sanam Industrial Group, affiliated with AIO, is involved in the manufacture of

---

[70] Souad Mekhennet and Joby Warrick, "Billion-dollar Sanctions-busting Scheme Aided Iran, Documents Show," *The Washington Post*, April 3, 2018.

[71] Adam Rawnsley, Betsy Woodruff, "Ukraine Intel: We Caught Iranians Smuggling a Ship-Killing Missile," *The Daily Beast*, March 30, 2018, https://www.thedailybeast.com/ukraine-intel-we-caught-iranians-smuggling-a-ship-killing-missile

non-military products, including household items, kitchen equipment, television sets, vacuum cleaners, washing machines, industrial fans, motor pumps, car parts, faucets, and parts and equipment for refineries and oil and gas pipes.[72]

Portions of factories belonging to Sanam Industrial Group are located at Parchin complex, which is an exclusively military complex. A front company for AIO purchases, importing required parts for the missile industry from foreign countries, Sanam works closely with all of the AIO missile factories. It also produces some military equipment and parts.

A large portion of the facility parts of Pars Oil and Gas Company are supplied by Sanam.

The Sanam factories have three divisions, which officially and openly produce non-military items. However, each of these divisions operates in line with a specific military initiative. These divisions are:

1. Sanam Alborz's official cover is the production of vacuum cleaners

2. Sanam Electronics' official cover is the manufacture of television sets, audio/visual equipment and electronic components. The division is responsible for building audio electronic equipment for AIO.

3. Sanam Oil group operates under the cover of procuring equipment for the oil and gas industry.

---

[72] "Sanam Industries Group," *Iran Watch*, https://www.iranwatch.org/iranian-entities/sanam-industries-group

Front companies to procure warheads

Similar to its nuclear activities, in order to advance its illicit missile purchases, the Iranian regime has attempted to set up front companies.

Asri New Technology Engineering (*Mohandesi Fanavari Novin Asri*) company is one of the most important front companies working to procure nuclear warheads.

In April 2007, the regime changed the name of this company to Advance Aerospace Technicians Company (*sherkate tows'eh fanavarane havapaye*) to prevent the identification of the company. This company is active in the design of warheads and other parts of missiles as well as in the illicit purchase of needed equipment for warhead production from other countries.

Mohsen Fakhrizadeh also registered Fash New Company for Processors (*Sherkat-e Novin Pardazeshgaran Fash*) on November 13, 2007. This company is involved in the import, export, sale installation, running, planning and repairing of all equipment related to computer networks, internet websites, hardware and software. These are utilized for missile warhead software.

MISSILE TESTS AND VIOLATIONS OF UNSC RESOLUTIONS

The Iranian regime's missile tests after the 2015 nuclear deal violate UNSC resolution 2231. The UN Secretary General highlighted these tests, stating in a July 12, 2016 report, six months after the implementation date of the JCPOA:

"22. On 28 March, I received a letter from France, Germany, the United Kingdom and the United States in which it was stressed that those launches were destabilizing, provocative and that they had been conducted in defiance of resolution 2231 (2015). Those States underscored that the phrase 'ballistic missiles designed to be capable of delivering nuclear weapons' in resolution 2231 (2015) included all Missile Technology Control Regime Category I systems, defined as those capable of delivering at least a 500 kg payload to a range of at least 300 km, which are inherently capable of delivering nuclear weapons and other weapons of mass destruction. Given that the Qiam-1 and Shahab-3 are Category I missiles, those States concluded that the launches of those missiles constituted an 'activity related to ballistic missiles designed to be capable of delivering nuclear weapons' and 'launches using such ballistic missile technology,' which the Islamic Republic of Iran has been called upon not to undertake pursuant to paragraph 3 of annex B to resolution 2231 (2015)."[73]

In response to protests by western countries, the Iranian regime claimed that the firing of ballistic missiles did not constitute a violation of the UNSC resolution.

In another part of the same report, which talks about the smuggling of RPG rockets and other weapons in violation of Resolution 2231 read:

"30. In its report, the United States indicated that it had seized an arms shipment from the Islamic Republic of Iran, which was likely bound for Yemen (see annex II). According to the report, on 28 March, a United States Navy ship boarded a dhow, the Adris, which was transiting international waters in the vicinity of the Gulf of Oman. That action, which the United States took in accordance with customary international law, as stated in its report, resulted in the discovery of a large weapons cache aboard the vessel, which included 1,500 Kalashnikov variant rifles, 200 RPG-7 and RPG-7V rocket-propelled grenade launchers and 21 DshK 12.7-mm machine guns (see fig. II). On the basis of an analysis of available information, including interviews with the crew and a review of the arms, the United States concluded that the arms had originated in the Islamic Republic of Iran and that their transfer was being undertaken contrary to paragraph 6 (b) of annex B to resolution 2231 (2015). After the weapons were seized, the dhow and its crew were allowed to depart."[74]

---

[73] "Report of the Secretary-General on the implementation of Security Council resolution 2231 (2015)," *United Nations Security Council,* July 12, 2016, http://www.securitycouncilreport.org/atf/cf/%7B65BFCF9B-6D27-4E9C-8CD3-CF6E4FF96FF9%7D/s_2016_589.pdf.

[74] Ibid.

On March 29, 2016, the U.S. Treasury placed sanctions on two companies, Nouri, and Movahed, both part of the Hemmat Missile Industrial Group involved in the building of ballistic missiles.[75] The companies were responsible for building warheads and final missile assembly respectively.

On January 25, 2018, a senior Iran analyst at the Foundation for Defense of Democracies in Washington, said in a report that since the July 2015 announcement of the nuclear deal, they have identified "as many as 23 ballistic missile launches by Iran."[76]

The report adds, "flight tests, even failed ones, teach Iran a great deal about the deficiencies in its missile arsenal. These missiles also bolster Iranian deterrence, providing Tehran with an umbrella of impunity that it uses to further its aggressive regional designs."[77]

According to the author of the report, Behnam Ben Taleblu, "even though the nuclear agreement itself does not directly address ballistic missiles, Iran's actions violate the UN Security Council resolution endorsing the JCPOA."[78]

According to the German Federal Intelligence Service, Iran has tried to engage large German companies to obtain advanced missile and weapons of mass destruction equipment, potential deals that

---

[75] "Treasury Sanctions Supporters of Iran's Ballistic Missile Program and Terrorism-Designated Mahan Air," March 24, 2016, https://www.treasury.gov/press-center/press-releases/Pages/jl0395.aspx.

[76] Behnam Ben Taleblu, "Iranian Ballistic Missile Tests Since the Nuclear Deal – 2.0," *Foundation For Defense of Democracies*, January 25, 2018, http://www.defenddemocracy.org/media-hit/behnam-ben-taleblu-iranian-ballistic-missile-tests-since-the-nuclear-deal-20/.

[77] Ibid.

[78] Behnam Ben Taleblu, "Iranian Ballistic Missile Tests Since the Nuclear Deal," *Foundation for Defense of Democracies*, 2017, http://www.defenddemocracy.org/content/uploads/documents/20917_Behnam_Ballistic_Missile.pdf

appear to be in violation of international agreements. Based on this report, Iran has enjoyed the assistance of a Chinese company.[79]

The report warned that "Iran's serious efforts to obtain scientific means and material to build WMD and missile technology," and stressed that "the Iranian regime has focused on German companies in all fields."

In one such example mentioned in the report, Iran has tried, through a Chinese company, to purchase a number of very advance systems to produce metal from a German engineering company. But, intelligence officials informed the said company of the details and prevented the sale of such equipment and their transfer to Iran.

Based on this report, German authorities have emphasized that Iran has always tried to purchase the equipment through a third country. This is the strategy that the regime continues to use to obtain raw material and banned equipment.

In January 2018, United Nations experts published their investigative report on the ballistic missiles attacks launched from Yemen.[80]

UN experts, who are responsible for monitoring the implementation of arms embargo on Yemen, were able to identify parts of the missile's casing and Yemeni drones that can be traced to Iran.[81]

---

[79] Benjamin Weinthal, "Iran Attempted to Buy Nuclear Technology Illegally 32 Times, German Agency Says," *Fox News*, October 9, 2017, http://www.foxnews.com/world/2017/10/09/iran-attempted-to-buy-nuclear-technology-illegally-32-times-german-agency-says.html.

[80] "UN: Iran Has Violated Arms Embargo in Yemen," *Euronews*, January 13, 2018, http://fa.euronews.com/2018/01/12/un-report-accuse-iran-to-violation-the-armes-embargo-in-yemen.

[81] Rick Gladstone, "Iran Violated Yemen Arms Embargo, U.N. Experts Say," The *New York Times*, January 12, 2018, https://www.nytimes.com/2018/01/12/world/middleeast/iran-yemen-saudi-arabia-arms-embargo-un.html

UN experts say that Iran has provided the possibility for the Houthis to use the regime's drones and ballistic missiles. Based on the report provided to the United Nations Security Council, Iran "is in non-compliance with paragraph 14 of resolution 2216 (2015)" related to arms embargo on Yemen.[82]

Without referring to the identity of the Iranian party, which was the source of the procurement and sending missile to the Houthis, the report emphasizes that Iran has not provided convincing answers to repeated requests by the experts at the end of 2017.

The report adds Tehran "failed to take the necessary measures to prevent the direct or indirect supply, sale or transfer, of Borkan-2H short-range ballistic missiles, filed storage tanks for liquid bi-propellant oxidizer for missiles and Ababil-T (Qasef-1) unmanned aerial vehicles, to the then Houthi-Saleh alliance."[83]

The United States, Britain, France and Germany issued a joint statement on February 27, 2018, condemning the Iranian regime's role in missile attacks conducted from Yemeni territory. The statement says, "These findings are of great concern. It is crucial that Iran does not carry out any action that is inconsistent with or would violate Security Council resolutions, and thereby risk destabilizing the security of the region and increasing the threat of broader conflict. We condemn such actions."[84]

---

[82] Richard Roth, "UN Report Accuses Iran and Saudis over Yemen," *CNN*, January 15, 2018, https://edition.cnn.com/2018/01/15/politics/un-report-iran-saudi-yemen/index.html.

[83] Ibid.

[84] "Joint Statement by France, Germany, the United Kingdom, and the United States," U.S. Embassy in Yemen, February 28, 2018, https://ye.usembassy.gov/pr-02282018/.

Despite such international condemnation, the Iranian regime continues to expand its missile activities. Brig. Gen. Amir Ali Hajizadeh, the Commander of the IRGC's Aerospace Force, said on March 7, 2018: "In the past, we had to offer a lot of explanations for such actions to many institutions. Now, however, that is not the case and our production has tripled compared to the past."[85]

---

[85] "Missile Production of Iran is up three folds," Interview with Hajizadeh, Farsi language, *Fars News Agency,* March 7, 2018, http://www.farsnews. com/newstext.php?nn=13961216000186

8

Vital Role
in Yemen
Based
Missile
Attacks

IRGC orders Houthi missile attack

The Houthis' firing of ballistic missiles against Saudi Arabia and the United Arab Emirates has become a major international issue. On December 14, 2017, US Ambassador to the UN Nikki Haley took part in a press conference in which she presented parts of the missiles that had been launched by the Houthis, and stated that the missiles were provided by the Iranian regime. Ambassador Haley presented documents on the launch of four missiles by the Houthis, which they had received from Iran. These included Qiam and Toufan missiles.

According to reports obtained by the Iranian Resistance from sources within the Iranian regime, more specifically from the Islamic Revolutionary Guard Corps (IRGC), all missile launches in the second half of 2017 by the Ansarallah militias (Houthis) in Yemen were carried out on the direct orders of the IRGC.

The IRGC command directed the Houthis to take retaliatory action against regional countries, particularly Saudi Arabia, in response to international and regional actions taken against the meddling of the IRGC and its proxy groups, such as Hezbollah.

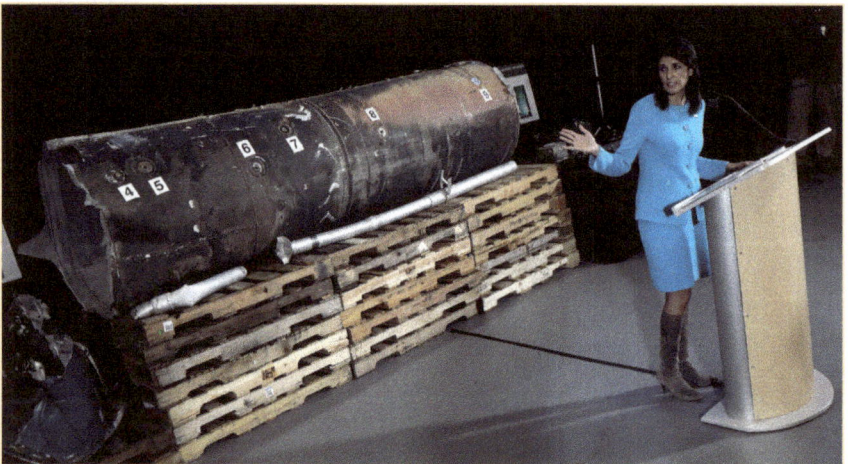

US Ambassador to the United Nations Nikki Haley: "In this warehouse is concrete evidence of illegal Iranian weapons proliferation, gathered from direct military attacks on partners in the region"

Based on these reports, the missiles are built by the IRGC's Aerospace Industries Organization and the IRGC and the Lebanese Hezbollah experts have trained the Houthis on how to use them.

At a press conference at the British Parliament on March 8, 2017, the Iranian Resistance revealed that the IRGC had set up a large number of front companies, through which it transferred ammunition to the regime's mercenaries, including in Yemen.[86]

The network of the opposition Mujahedin-e Khalq (MEK) inside Iran has identified several shipping companies for smuggling weapons, especially to Yemen. According to the reports, these companies had previously smuggled weapons to Yemen directly, but after the closure of direct sea routes to Yemen in 2015, they have circumvented the sanctions through other ports in the region. Among these companies, Valfajr is affiliated to Khatam Al-Anbia Construction Headquarters, which ships different types of cargo for the IRGC by smuggling or transferring goods. This company's ships use non-Iranian flags to avoid being identified or raise suspicious.

Qiam and Toufan missiles

The Qiam Missile is a variant of the Scud Missile, which is known in Iran as Shahab 2. This is a ballistic missile using liquid fuel and manufactured and assembled by the Hemmat Industrial Group. However, parts of this missile are produced in Bagheri Industry, Bakeri Industrial Group and Ya-Mehdi Industrial Group. The Iranian regime previously purchased Scud-C missiles from North Korea, but it started assembling them in Iran with the help of North Korea and renamed it Shahab 2.[87] Qiam Missile is

[86] "Arab Media Coverage Of Iran Opposition Unveiling IRGC Activities In London Press Conference," NCRI-US, March 12, 2017, goo.gl/LkMKn5

[87] Paul K. Kerr, Steven A. Hildreth, Mary Beth D. Nikitin, "Iran-North Korea-Syria Ballistic Missile and Nuclear Cooperation," *Congressional Research*

an enhanced version of Shahab 2 Missile. Its range has increased from 500 to 800 km. The enhanced model does not have the small wings and was made public for the first time in 2012.

The Toufan Missile is a variant of the TOW Missile and is produced by the Ya Mahdi Industrial Group.

Shahid Bagheri Industries

The Qiam missile actuator could be seen in some of the pieces made of cast iron, marked with "Shahid Bagheri Industry" logo with the abbreviation S.B.I. Shahid Bagheri Industries is one of the oldest IRGC and Defense Ministry's missile manufacturing units where, in the past, the assembly of the "Shahab" ballistic missiles were finalized.[88] According to reports, in 1997, Hassan Tehrani Moghaddam, an IRGC Commander and the main architect of regime's missile system (killed in a missile explosion at the Modarres Garrison near Tehran in 2011), was commissioning the final assembly of the Shahab 3 missile in these factories.[89]

However, in the years since, with the development of the missile industry, changes were made to the mandate of the Bagheri Industries.

At present, Bagheri Industries is one of the subsidiaries of "Shahid Ahmad Kazemi Group Industries" or the "Aerospace Group Industries," which produces various types of smaller size

---

Service, February 26, 2016 https://fas.org/sgp/crs/nuke/R43480.pdf

[88] An actuator is a mechanical device that moves and controls a mechanism that is indented for use in missile or rocket applications, or in the launch systems supporting the flight operations of these platforms. https://www.thomasnet.com/products/actuators-301168-1.html

[89] John W. Parker, "Russia and the Iranian Nuclear Program: Replay or Breakthrough?" *Institute for National Strategic Studies,* March 2012, https://www.files.ethz.ch/isn/143232/Strategic-Perspectives-9.pdf

and surface-to-surface missiles, namely Fajr 1, 2 and 3, and Falaq 1 and 2 missiles. These missiles are delivered by the IRGC to regional proxy groups such as Lebanon's Hezbollah.[90] The plant also produces parts for ballistic missiles, including the "Qiam" missile.

The industry has three factories in three different locations.

A part of the Bagheri Industries is located inside the Parchin site and in the air defense complex called Parchin 10. (Its general position has been marked in the aerial photo of Parchin site below).

The location of another factory of Bagheri Industries in Tehran is next to the Sepenta factories at Shahid Bagheri Street, 9 km into the Fath Highway. The regime's public websites describe the work of this factory as "Manufacturing parts and systems of power plants, and a variety of industrial high-pressure valves, high-pressure pumps and pressure vessels," which are a cover

A part of the Bagheri Industries is located at Plan 10 of the Parchin military complex

---

[90] Anthony H. Cordesman, "Iran's Rocket and Missile Forces and Strategic Options," *Center for Strategic and International Studies*, October 7, 2014, https://csis-prod.s3.amazonaws.com/s3fs-public/legacy_files/files/publication/141007_Iran_Rocket_Missile_forces.pdf

One factory of Bagheri Industries in Tehran is next to the Sepenta factories at Shahid Bagheri Street

for the real activities the plant. Hall 15 of this plant was the site for the final assembly of the Shahab missile in 1997.

Another factory of Bagheri Industries in Tehran is situated in kilometer 17 of Karaj Road - across from Darou Pakhsh Street.

The "design and manufacturing of machines for the production and printing of cardboard boxes" are described as the factory's output, which is a cover for the activities of this plant to build missile components.

Another factory of Bagheri Industries in Tehran is in km 17 of Karaj Road

9

Conclusion and the Way Forward

The clerical regime claims that its missile program is purely defensive in nature and is primarily an instrument of deterrence. From this line of logic, it follows that the state has every right to expand the program. However, the current report demonstrates that the regime's missile program is not principally defensive. In order to better comprehend this line of reasoning, the program must be examined and scrutinized in the larger context of the regime's overall policies and objectives.

Much like its nuclear program, the regime's missile arsenal must be studied in the context of its systematic policy of exporting terrorism and fundamentalism, with the explicit intention of establishing a "Union of Islamic Republics," rhetorical aspirations of which have been codified in the regime's constitution. The preamble of the Iranian regime's constitution refers to the IRGC's mandate of "extending the sovereignty of God's law throughout the world" ... "with the hope that this century will witness the establishment of a universal holy government."

The regime has an arsenal of missiles with a range of 2,000 km, which it has built up with all its might and resolve thanks to the western policy of appeasement throughout the previous decades. The regime intends to create a safe geopolitical passage from Tehran to the Mediterranean shores in Lebanon and Syria in order to extend instability to the region and territories beyond the Middle East, including vast parts of Europe, as well as American bases.

By extending its dominance over significant portions of Yemen, Tehran threatens one of the main waterways in the world. The Yemeni Houthis' repeated firing of missiles provided to them by the clerical regime is one actualized instance of this threat, which leaves no doubt about the Iranian regime's destructive regional role. Major General Hassan Firouzabadi, the regime's former chairman of the joint chiefs of staff, said on November 12, 2016: "If the Leader [Khamenei] permits, missiles will be launched. Otherwise, they will not be launched. Even the time of the launch is determined by him."[91]

The regime's nuclear and missiles program, joined with its regional meddling, is a telltale sign of its strategic vulnerability and desperate attempts to continue its survival. That is why even as it oversees economic ruin compounded by major fiscal constraints, and despite international objections, the regime continues its missiles program while risking more economic sanctions. Importantly, despite their internal disputes and conflicts over power sharing arrangements within the system, all of the regime's influential factions are united and in virtual agreement over the missile program precisely because they see the program as a vital component for the regime's survival.

The mass popular uprising against the regime that enveloped the country in December 2017 and January 2018 infused the biggest shock to the ruling theocracy, raising the real and viable prospect of its downfall. This, in turn, has increased the regime's need to expand and enlarge the scope of its missile program in conjunction with its regional meddling.

The policy of appeasement and pacifism, long practised by major players in the international community, particularly the unjustified western concessions to the regime during the nuclear negotiations, convinced the mullahs that they can continue their malign regional adventurism with virtual impunity. This broadly conciliatory policy vis-à-vis the clerical regime acted as a decisive element in spawning the current regional crises, including most prominently the wars in Yemen and Syria, the

---

[91] "Firouzabdi: No missile are launched unless approved by the Supreme Leader," *EuroNews,* November 12, 2016, http://fa.euronews.com/2016/11/12/iran-firouzabadi-said-missile-firing-need-to-confirm-supreme-leader

latter of which has left over 500,000 people dead so far. The regime's advances in this arena are not a sign of its strength but the symptom of a weak and indecisive posture from the U.S. and Europe in relation to Tehran.

The Iranian theocracy will not abandon these policies for as long as it possibly can because these strategies are inextricably linked to its survival. The regime's supreme leader Ali Khamenei explicitly stated on May 10, 2017: "there is no difference between change of behavior and change of regime."[92] The hypothesis that the regime will eventually desert these policies is only conceivable in the context of zero compromise with Tehran, zero concessions, and zero loopholes. Any new measures, resolutions or executive orders should include the regime's cruise missiles, as the range is long and the payload is good enough to be capable of carrying a nuclear warhead.

The mullahs' missile program must be terminated, period. On the backdrop of the regime's current circumstances, particularly after the start of recent mass uprisings in Iran, the mullahs are in their most weakened state, which means that the regime is at its most vulnerable juncture.

Experience has shown repeatedly that the way to resolving the current crises in the region, which have the regime as their chief instigator, lies only in regime change at the hands of the Iranian people and their organized resistance. For its part, the international community must shift its policies to exhibiting resolve and firmness, not appeasement and conciliation, vis-à-vis Tehran in order to arrest the spread of more damaging crises around the region.

---

92 Majid Rafizadeh, "Iran Has Accelerated Its Missile Activities," *Huffington Post,* June 20, 2017, https://www.huffingtonpost.com/entry/iran-has-accelerated-its-missile-activities_us_5949bf2de4b0710bea889a60

10

Glossary

Aerospace Industries Organization (AIO) — Responsible for the manufacturing of advanced missiles and other military industrial equipment and products. Also responsible for the production of surface-to-air missiles, surface-to-surface missiles, missiles launched from submarines, surface-to-sea missiles, sea-to-surface missiles as well as rockets and explosives, missile launch pads, gyroscopes and other equipment.

Ballistic Missile — an object that is forcibly propelled at a target, either by hand or from a mechanical weapon with a high, arching trajectory, that is initially powered and guided but falls under gravity onto its target.

Deterrence — The concept that supports the use of fear and retaliation to discourage action.

International Atomic Energy Agency (IAEA) — The International Atomic Energy Agency is an international organization, affiliated with the United Nations that strives to promote the prohibition of the use of nuclear weapons and to maintain peace in the presence of nuclear energy.

Islamic Revolutionary Guard Corps (IRGC) — A paramilitary organization within the Iranian regime, created by then Supreme Leader Khomeini to uphold and maintain the regime in power.

Iraq-Iran War — A conflict between Iran and Iraq, beginning in late 1980 and ending under a ceasefire in 1988. This lead to the IRGC to pursue ballistic missile in attempt to end the stalemate.

Joint Comprehensive Plan of Action (JCPOA) — An agreement reached on July 14, 2015 on behalf of the participation of the United States of America, Iran, United

Kingdom, France, Germany, Russia, and China intended to monitor Iran's nuclear program.

Organization of Defensive Innovation and Research (or the Farsi acronym SPND) — The engineering unit controlled by the military and tasked with the development of nuclear weapons inside the Iranian regime. It is headed by Mohsen Fakhrizadeh Mahabadi, also known as Dr. Hassan Mohseni, a veteran IRGC brigadier general and the key figure in the regime's nuclear weapons program.

United Nations Security Council (UNSC) — One of the voting bodies of the United Nations comprising of 5 permanent members and 10 rotating members.

Raison D'être- The most important reason or purpose for someone or something's existence

Weapons of Mass Destruction — Weapons intended for large-scale violence and death. Can be biological, radioactive, or chemical weaponry.

Yemeni Houthis — Main Rebel group in Yemen also known as Ansarallah militias, that receives a great deal of monetary and military support from the Iranian regime, including ballistic missiles.

11

Appendices

APPENDIX A: NOTABLE NUCLEAR AND MISSILE REVELATIONS OF THE IRANIAN RESISTANCE (1991-2017)

Since 1991 the Iranian resistance has exposed more than 100 secret nuclear projects of the Iranian regime. Some of the more notable nuclear revelations include:

1. **June 1991:** Revealing the regime's preliminary nuclear facilities in Mo'alm Kalaye.

2. **October 1992:** Revealing the attempt to purchase nuclear warheads from Kazakhstan. The revelation aborted the shipment of the warheads to Iran.

3. **January 1998:** Revealing the advancement of Shahab-3 missiles and that the work on the missile is completed and that Iran is ready for production.

4. **August 2002:** Revealing the uranium enrichment facility in Natanz, being the largest and most expansive of the regime's investment on its nuclear weapons program in a press

conference in Washington, DC. The revelation disrupted Tehran's nuclear calculations and led IAEA inspections to Iran that confirmed the revelation;

5. **August 14, 2002:** Revealing the heavy water project in Arak in a press conference in Washington, DC.

6. **February 2003:** Revealing the most important companies involved in producing and importing equipment and necessary material for nuclear projects, including Kala Electric in Aab-Ali highway that was registered as a watch-making factory. However, this was actually a center for centrifuge assembly and testing, and in an IAEA inspection, traces of highly enriched uranium were found at this site.

7. **May 2003:** Revealing the Lavizan-Shian Center. This was a very sensitive nuclear site for the regime and the mullahs immediately destroyed it and even removed the soil before allowing a June 2004 IAEA visit to the site.

8. **October 2003:** Revealing the Lashkarabad site and its front company (May 2003). This site was inspected by the IAEA, and the regime deceived the inspectors by taking them to another location.

9. **November 2003:** Revealing in November 2003, the special role of the IRGC in the nuclear projects clearly showed the military goals and aspects of this project.

10. **April 2004:** The NCRI revealed that Tehran had dedicated 400 nuclear experts to military industries.

11. **April 2004:** Exposing the new Center for Readiness and New Defense Technology (Lavizan-2). The equipment and activities from razed Lavizan site was moved to this site, but the site was kept off limits.

12. **September 2004:** NCRI revealed the allotment of $16bn to nuclear technology, purchase and smuggling of Deuterium from Russia, as well as details on the AEOI's companies;

13. **November 2004:** Revealing in a press conference in Paris the new technology center (Mojdeh site) and the names of their experts. In the conference, the Iranian resistance revealed the identity of Mohsen Fakhrizadeh, the key man of Iranian clandestine nuclear program who was kept secret until then. The IAEA has been insisting to interview Fakhrizaeh for the past few years, but the Iranian regime has not provided access.

14. **December 2004:** Revealing the Hemmat Missile Industries site in relation to produce nuclear chemical warheads.

15. **December 2004:** Revealing ongoing research and ground testing of the Ghadr-1 missile.

16. **February 2005:** Revealing a project aimed at producing polonium-210 and beryllium to build nuclear bomb fuses.

17. **March 2005:** Revealing the secret nuclear center in the Parchin tunnel. This site focused on laser enrichment.

18. **May 2005:** Revealing the production and importing graphite necessary for nuclear bomb production.

19. **July 2005:** Revealing the import and production of Maraging steel to build the bomb fuselage and using it in centrifuge systems.

20. **August 2005:** Revealing the production of 4,000 ready-to-install centrifuges.

21. **August 2005:** Revealing in a press conference in Washington, DC, the meeting between Abdul Qadeer Khan, and

commanders of the Iranian Revolutionary Guards in 1986 and 1987 in Tehran.

22. **August 2005:** Revealing in a press conference in Brussels the regime's plans to smuggle tritium from South Korea to increase nuclear explosion power.

23. **September 2005:** Revealing, in a Washington, DC, press conference, the regime's tunnel construction in its military centers to keep secret the material and equipment.

24. **September 2005:** Revealing in a press conference in Vienna that North Korean experts were helping the Iranian regime in developing warheads in Hemmat site in Khojir region, southeast of Tehran.

25. **November 2005:** In a press conference in Vienna, the NCRI revealed that the Iranian regime had taken the IAEA inspectors to another location than the one the UN nuclear watchdog was looking for at the sprawling Parchin military site.

26. **November 2005:** In a Washington, DC, press conference in, the NCRI revealed that Iran was building nuclear capable missiles in underground secret tunnels.

27. **December 2005:** In a press conference in Paris, the NCRI revealed the construction of a series of secret new sites, including one in Qom. Four years later it was established that site was Ferdow clandestine site, used for enriching uranium.

28. **January 2006:** Revealing importing of industrial press machines to shape enriched uranium in a bomb.

29. **March 2006:** Exposing that the regime has ramped up its development of the Ghadr-1, 70 percent complete.

30. **August 2006:** Revealing the production of P2 centrifuges.

31. **September 2006:** Revealing in Washington, DC, the reactivation of laser enrichment projects.

32. **February 2007:** Revealing the specifications of 7 nuclear front companies related to the nuclear fuel cycle.

33. **September 2007:** Revealing a secret tunnel being constructed by the Ministry of Defense south of the Natanz site.

34. **February 2008:** Revealing the location of nuclear warhead construction in Khojeir and the nuclear weapon command center in Mojdeh.

35. **March 2008:** Revealing Beheshti University as a nuclear research center related to commanding weapons production in Mojdeh.

36. **September 2009:** Revealing Center of Explosion and Impact Technology (METFAZ) and changes in the nuclear command center.

37. **October 2009:** Revealing further details about the Fordow site.

38. **September 2010:** In Washington, D.C., the NCRI revealed a covert nuclear site located in tunnels in Behjatabad in the Abyek Township of Qazvin Province. This covert nuclear site was codenamed "311" and is known as Javadinia 2;

39. **April 2011:** The NCRI revealed in Washington, DC, the covert site near Tehran, named TABA, which was involved in production of centrifuge parts for tens of thousands of centrifuges. Tehran conceded the existence of this site the next day;

40. **July 2011:** Revealing in Washington, DC, the Defensive Innovation and Research Organization (SPND) nuclear bomb

command center chaired by Mohsen Fakhrizadeh. SPND was later sanctioned by the Department of State in August 2014.

41. **January 2012:** Revealing 100 names of nuclear engineering experts active in various bomb making sections.

42. **April 2012:** Revealing in Washington, DC, further details of SPND operations, its involvement in the Fordow site, and the list of experts associated with this center.

43. **July 2013:** Revealing the top-secret Maadan Sharq nuclear site in Tehran's Damavand district.

44. **October 2013:** Revealing the relocation of Defensive Innovation and Research Organization (SPND) nuclear bomb command center.

45. **November 2013:** Revealing the "012" secret site in Isfahan's Mobarakeh linked to SPND.

46. **November 2014:** In a Washington, DC conference, revealing the Iranian regime's activities related to high explosive chambers at Parchin military site.

47. **February 2015:** Revealing in a press conference in Washington, DC, the existence of Lavizan-3 underground nuclear site in Tehran.

48. **May 2015:** NCRI Paris Office revealed the cooperation between the Iranian regime and North Korea regarding the nuclear weapons program of Iran and the presence of North Korean nuclear scientists in Tehran.

49. **June 2015:** Revealing Iran's deceitful tactics during nuclear negotiations with the P 5+1.

50. **September 2015:** Revealing Iran's cooperation with North Korea to deceive IAEA inspectors.

51. **December 2015:** Revealing how Iran laid out a plan to deceive the IAEA in its probe of Possible Military Dimensions of Iran's nuclear program.

52. **April 2017:** Revealing in press conference in Washington, DC, the status of the Iranian regime's nuclear bomb making apparatus, Plan-6 in the Parchin military complex operated by SPND.

53. **June 2017:** Revealing dozens of missile centers across Iran, including those which work in close collaboration with the nuclear bomb-making entity, SPND.

APPENDIX B: PUBLICATIONS

List of Publications by the National Council of Resistance of Iran, U.S. Representative Office

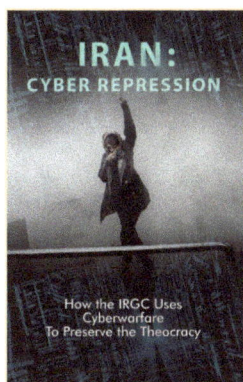

Iran: Cyber Repression: How the IRGC Uses Cyberwarfare to Preserve the Theocracy
February 2018, 70 pages

This manuscript demonstrates how the Iranian regime, under the supervision and guidance of the IRGC and the Ministry of Intelligence and Security (MOIS), have employed new cyberwarfare and tactics in a desperate attempt to counter the growing dissent inside the country.

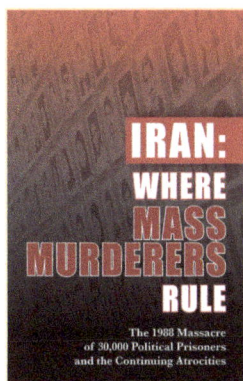

Iran: Where Mass Murderers Rule:
The 1988 Massacre of 30,000 Political Prisoners and the Continuing Atrocities
November 2017, 161 pages

Iran: Where Mass Murderers Rule is an expose of the current rulers of Iran and their track record in human rights violations. The book details how 30,000 political prisoners fell victim to politicide during the summer of 1988 and showcases the most egregious political extinction of a group of people.

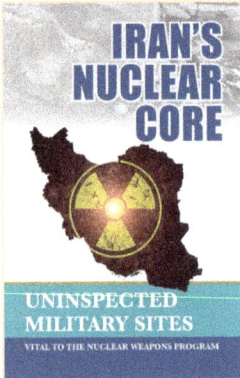

Iran's Nuclear Core: Uninspected Military Sites, Vital to the Nuclear Weapons Program
October 2017, 52 pages

This book details how the nuclear weapons program is at the heart, and not in parallel, to the civil nuclear program of Iran. The program has been run by the Islamic Revolution- ary Guards Corp (IRGC) since the beginning, and the main nuclear sites and nuclear research facilities have been hidden from the eyes of the United Nations nuclear watchdog.

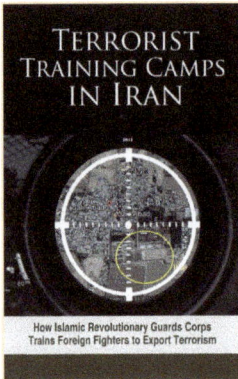

Terrorist Training Camps in Iran: How Islamic Revolutionary Guards Corps Trains Foreign Fighters to Export Terrorism
June 1017, 56 pages

The book details how Islamic Revolutionary Guards Corps trains foreign fighters in 15 various camps in Iran to export terrorism. The IRGC has created a large directorate within its extraterritorial arm, the Quds Force, in order to expand its training of foreign mercenaries as part of the strategy to step up its meddling abroad in Syria, Iraq, Yemen, Bahrain, Afghanistan and elsewhere.

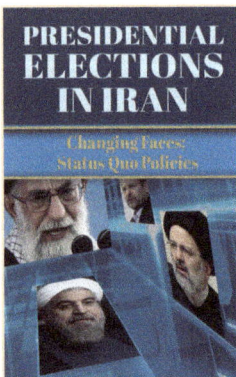

Presidential Elections in Iran: Changing Faces; Status Quo Policies
May 2017, 78 pages

The book, reviews the past 11 presidential elections, demonstrating that the only criterion for qualifying as a candidate is practical and heartfelt allegiance to the Supreme Leader. An unelected vetting watchdog, the Guardian Council makes that determination.

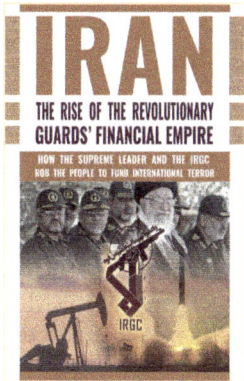

The Rise of Iran's Revolutionary Guards' Financial Empire: How the Supreme Leader and the IRGC Rob the People to Fund International Terror
March 2017, 174 pages

This manuscript examines some vital factors and trends, including the overwhelming and accelerating influence (especially since 2005) of the Supreme Leader and the Islamic Revolutionary Guard Corps (IRGC). This study shows how ownership of property in various spheres of the economy is gradually shifted from the population writ large towards a minority ruling elite comprised of the Supreme Leader's office and the IRGC, using 14 powerhouses, and how the money ends up funding terrorism worldwide.

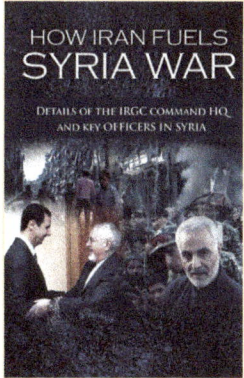

How Iran Fuels Syria War: Details of the IRGC Command HQ and Key Officers in Syria
November 2016, 74 pages

This book examines how the Iranian regime has effectively engaged in the military occupation of Syria by marshaling 70,000 forces, including the Islamic Revolutionary Guard Corps (IRGC) and mercenaries from other countries into Syria; is paying monthly salaries to over 250,000 militias and agents to prolong the conflict; divided the country into 5 zones of conflict and establishing 18 command, logistics and operations centers.

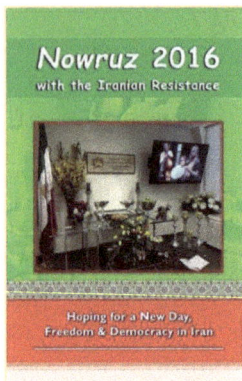

Nowruz 2016 with the Iranian Resistance: Hoping for a New Day, Freedom and Democracy in Iran
April 2016, 36 pages

This book describes Iranian New Year, Nowruz celebrations at the Washington office of Iran's parliament-in-exile, the National Council of Resistance of Iran. The yearly event marks the beginning of spring. It includes select speeches by dignitaries who have attended the NCRIUS Nowruz celebrations. This book also discusses the very rich culture and the traditions associated with Nowruz for centuries.

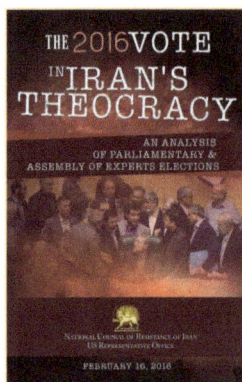

The 2016 Vote in Iran's Theocracy: An analysis of Parliamentary & Assembly of Experts Elections
February 2016, 70 pages

This book examines all the relevant data about the 2016 Assembly of Experts as well as Parliamentary elections ahead of the February 2016 elections. It looks at the history of elections since the revolution in 1979 and highlights the current intensified infighting among the various factions of the Iranian regime.

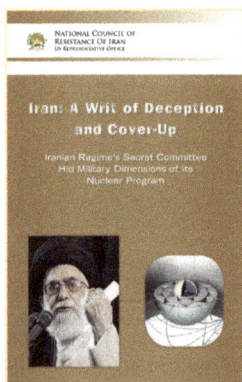

IRAN: A Writ of Deception and Cover-up: Iranian Regime's Secret Committee Hid Military Dimensions of its Nuclear Program
February 2016, 30 pages

The book provides details about a top-secret committee in charge of forging the answers to the International Atomic Energy Agency

(IAEA) regarding the Possible Military Dimensions (PMD) of Tehran's nuclear program, including those related to the explosive detonators called EBW (Exploding Bridge Wire) detonator, which is an integral part of a program to develop an implosion type nuclear device.

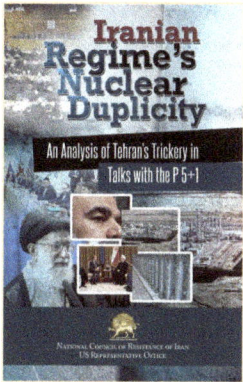

Iranian Regime's Nuclear Duplicity: An Analysis of Tehran's Trickery in Talks with the P 5+1

January 2016, 74 pages

This book examines Iran's behavior throughout the negotiations process in an effort to inform the current dialogue on a potential agreement. Drawing on both publicly available sources and those within Iran, the book focuses on two major periods of intense negotiations with the regime: 2003-2004 and 2013-2015. Based on this evidence, it then extracts the principles and motivations behind Tehran's approach to negotiations as well as the tactics used to trick its counterparts and reach its objectives.

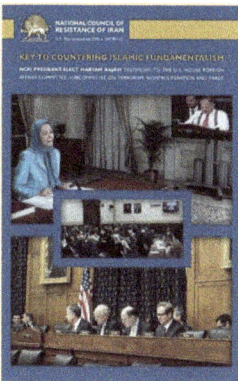

Key to Countering Islamic Fundamentalism: Maryam Rajavi? Testimony To The U.S. House Foreign Affairs Committee

June 2015, 68 pages

Testimony before U.S. House Foreign Affairs Committee's subcommittee on Terrorism, non-Proliferation, and Trade discussing ISIS and Islamic fundamentalism. The book contains Maryam Rajavi's full testimony as well as the question and answer by representatives.

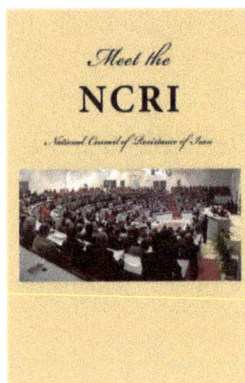

Meet the National Council of Resistance of Iran
June 2014, 150 pages

Meet the National Council of Resistance of Iran discusses what NCRI stands for, what its platform is, what it has done so far, and why a vision for a free, democratic, secular, non-nuclear republic in Iran would serve the world peace.

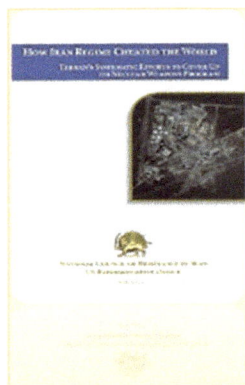

How Iran Regime Cheated the World:
Tehran's Systematic Efforts to Cover Up its Nuclear Weapons Program
June 2014, 50 pages

This book deals with one of the most fundamental challenges that goes to the heart of the dispute regarding the Iranian regime's controversial nuclear program: to ascertain with certainty that Tehran will not pursue a nuclear bomb. Such an assurance can only be obtained through specific steps taken by Tehran in response to the international community's concerns. The monograph discusses the Iranian regime's report card as far as it relates to being transparent when addressing the international community's concerns about the true nature and the ultimate purpose of its nuclear program

APPENDIX C: ABOUT NCRI-US

National Council of Resistance of Iran-US Representative Office acts as the Washington office for Iran's Parliament-in-exile, which is dedicated to the establishment of a democratic, secular, non-nuclear republic in Iran.

NCRI-US, registered as a non-profit tax-exempt organization, has been instrumental in exposing the nuclear weapons program of Iran, including the sites in Natanz, and Arak, the biological and chemical weapons program of Iran, as well as its ambitious ballistic missile program.

NCRI-US has also exposed the terrorist network of the Iranian regime, including its involvement in the bombing of Khobar Towers in Saudi Arabia, the Jewish Community Center in Argentina, its fueling of sectarian violence in Iraq and Syria, and its malign activities in other parts of the Middle East.

Our office has provided information on the human rights violations in Iran, extensive anti-government demonstrations, and the movement for democratic change in Iran.

Visit our website at **www.ncrius.org**

You may follow us on   **twitter**   @ncrius

Follow us on   **facebook**   NCRIUS

You can also find us on   **Instagram**   NCRIUS